Happiness Is No Secret

Happiness Is NO SECRET

Bob C. Hardison

BROADMAN PRESS
Nashville, Tennessee

Unless otherwise indicated, all Scripture references are from the
King James Version of the Holy Bible.
The quotation marked (RSV) is from the Revised Standard Version
of the Bible, copyrighted 1946, 1952, © 1971, 1973.
The quotations marked (TLB) are from *The Living Bible, Para-
phrased* (Wheaton, IL: Tyndale House Publishers, 1971) and are
used by permission.

Library of Congress Cataloging-in-Publication Data

Hardison, Bob C., 1947-
  Happiness is no secret.

  1. Happiness. 2. Interpersonal relations.
3. Contentment. I. Title.
BF575.H27H37 1987   158   87-11675
ISBN 0-8054-5051-3 (pbk.)

To the members of First Baptist Church, Sebree, Kentucky, whose prayerful support has meant more to me than I can ever express

and

to my wise father, A. B. Hardison,

and

to my loving mother, Blanche Johnston, this book is affectionately dedicated.

Bob C. Hardison

Acknowledgments

Much of the material used in this book I have gleaned from years of Bible study. Where I could, I have given the sources for the ideas and illustrations. I am indebted to many friends, pastors, and writers too numerous to mention. Two have been especially helpful: Dr. Wayne Dehoney and Dr. Frank Pollard. Their sermons in *The Pulpit of Walnut Street Baptist* in Louisville and *The Baptist Hour*, respectively, have been rich resource material.

I wish to thank Miss Laura McElroy and Mrs. Lee (Tommy Ann) Rosenzweig for typing this material. Also, I thank my wife, Violet, for being an invaluable asset as a proofreader. Furthermore, I wish to thank the congregations of Friendship Baptist in Modesto, California, Calvary Baptist in Nashville, Tennessee, and First Baptist in Sebree, Kentucky, for allowing me to be their pastor. I have learned much more from them than they have learned from me.

Introduction
Where Is Happyville?

Hapeville is the name of a town near Atlanta, Georgia. Not knowing the correct pronunciation, a stranger asked an Atlanta mail carrier, "Where is Happyville?" "I wish I knew!" the mail carrier exclaimed.

Can you identify with those feelings? Do you wish you knew where to find happiness? Many strive for it and never quite attain it.

Some people think happiness is suddenly found as a discovery. They see it as the good fortune of a child who finds the prize egg in the Easter egg hunt. So they are looking to find sudden happiness in a new girl friend, a winning lottery ticket, or an early retirement. No sudden discovery is going to swap misery, maladjustment, frustration, and emptiness for happiness. No, it simply doesn't work that way. You won't all at once slip up on happiness or accidently discover it.

You can't just pursue happiness in and of itself and have it. It won't work just to clench your fist and say, "I'm tired of being miserable! I'm going to make myself be happy!" No way. It's like a dog chasing its tail. The harder he chases it, the more exhausted he gets, and he never catches it.

Sadly enough, few people have found true happiness. Husbands fight with their wives, employees gripe about their jobs. Even the sad faces of church people are poor advertisements for the abundant joy found in the Christian life.

For most folks, happiness is very illusive. They momentarily grasp it, then lose it. Others never experience it at all. Yet, happiness isn't a secret. No matter how unhappy you are now, or have been in the past, you can start experiencing happiness.

You begin to experience happiness when you start doing certain things to make happiness come. It will come to you as a by-product as you incorporate these elements into your life.

Happiness is no secret! I am experiencing it, and you can, too. Are you ready? Let's go! Turn these pages to learn the elements that will bring about happiness in your life.

Contents

1.

The Real You Is
Trying to Come Out
A Good Self-Image

Comedian Rodney Dangerfield with his big eyes and "hang-dog" look can make a living complaining, "I get no respect!" But, aren't the rest of us good at destroying ourselves, too? Have you ever said, "I'm just good for nothing," "Nobody loves me," or "Nobody appreciates me"?

Your mate forgets your anniversary. You feel slighted and begin to sull up. At work you are slighted. It's promotion time, and you are overlooked. You think, *My company doesn't appreciate me!* The boss doesn't comment on your work, and you feel ignored. Very soon you begin feeling you aren't worth much.

As a child, you may have been called "Fatso," "Peanut Brain," "Big Ox," or something just as hurting. Your peers made fun of you. Your parents sounded like a drill sergeant snapping out one command after another: "Cut your nails," "Quit chewing that gum like that," "Turn off the TV," or, "Why do you wear that?" Verbal abuse has added negative stroke upon negative stroke until you feel unattractive and stupid.

As a member of a publishing company's editorial advisory board, Kenneth Chafin receives a copy of each of their books.

One day while thumbing through the new books, he found one that had left page 67 blank. Just as he had noticed it, a student came into his office. Chafin said, "Would you look at this! I got this book, and page 67 is blank!" The student looked at it a moment and replied, "I know just how page 67 feels." Chafin thought the student was melodramatic and ushered him out.

A couple of months later Chafin taught a Bible study at Laity Lodge. He told one of his groups about the student identifying with a blank page. They laughed. Then at coffee break, one by one, they all came around and said, "I know how that student feels." They told about a brother who was so talented or a sister who made all *A's*. Some mentioned a cousin who did everything or a parent who was "perfect." Chafin was amazed at how many of them thought there was nothing good about themselves. They thought everyone else was gifted and talented, but when it came to themselves, they were page 67![1]

A healthy attitude about yourself is a major factor in happiness. Self-acceptance is so terribly important. It does not guarantee happiness, but it does play an important role.

What you think about yourself subconsciously influences how you react to specific situations. Thoughts are transformed into actions. A young person who is gifted in sports plays football but not basketball. Why? Because he feels too conspicuous out on the basketball court. It isn't that he doesn't have as much ability to play basketball as he does football. It's just that he can put on the helmet and pads and play without feeling like everyone is looking at him. A poor self-image will keep you from attempting new challenges.

Low self-esteem will enslave you. It will stifle your problem-solving ability. Instead of confronting your problems and dealing with them forthrightly, you will avoid or put off the things that bother you. Low self-esteem will hold you down throughout life unless you work to change it.

Contrary to common belief you can change your self-image.

You may lack self-confidence because of previous failures or mistakes. Your deprived childhood may have given you an inferiority complex. A divorce may have left you feeling ugly and unwanted. But you don't have to continue under those dark clouds.

Cristy Lane is now a prominent country music star. In 1979, she was voted Top New Female Artist by the Academy of Country Music. Her record of "One Day at a Time" has sold more albums than any other Gospel record and is still selling at a rapid pace. Cristy is poised and outgoing, but she has not always had such an air of self-confidence.

Cristy Lane was not always well off or famous. She was born Eleanor (Ellie) Johnston, the eighth of twelve children of Andrew and Pansy Johnston in East Peoria, Illinois. Ellie's childhood was warm and secure until one night during her sophomore year in high school. She was to sing with the school choir before her first live audience. Her mother had made over one of her older sister's dresses. It looked brand-new. Even though the teacher had told them all to wear white dresses, this one would have to do. After all, the polka dots were small— hardly noticeable!

The auditorium was filled. Ellie hurried to take her place in line with the rest of her classmates. Ready to perform they all stood quietly behind the red, heavily worn drapes. The teacher inspected the children. Eyeing Ellie intently, she began shaking her head. With disgust she barked, "You don't really think you're going on stage dressed like that, do you?"

"Ma'am?"

"You were told to wear a white dress."

"It's my sister's dress, ma'am," she stammered. "We couldn't afford a new one. It's the best my mother had."

"I distinctly said 'an all-white dress,'" the teacher scolded. "This won't do at all. You're excused. Someone else will sing your part."

Blinded by tears, Ellie turned and stumbled from the stage through the exit, into the night. She thought silently, *I will never go on a stage! They can have their old music! I will never sing again!*

One day, years later, she was at the sink peeling carrots for dinner, watching the children play in the backyard. Ellie thought, *What a beautiful day it is*. Lee Stoller, her husband, was in the living room watching the Yankees and Dodgers battle it out for the 1965 World Series.

Idly, she began to sing . . .

"Honey, who was that singing on the radio?" Lee asked. Shyly she answered, "Nobody! It was me!" Lee stared at her in disbelief. He had never heard her sing. He didn't even know she could. Amazed at her beautiful voice he got her to sing again. Lee recorded her and worked with building her self-confidence until she began singing in night clubs and county fairs. As her promoter and companion, Lee urged her to become a country music star.[2]

Ellie Johnston Stoller (Cristy Lane) didn't stay a crushed little girl under the dark clouds of rejection. She, through much effort, changed her feelings of inadequacy. And you can, too. It's up to you! To improve your self-image you can work on these things.

Recognize Your Infinite Worth

A good place to begin is to recognize your infinite worth. One day while I was listening to Teddy Bart's afternoon talk program on WSM Radio in Nashville, Tennessee, a woman came on the air. "This morning before my husband went to work he told me he didn't love me. He has been living with me only because of the children. I am crushed!"

"Without knowing more," Bart replied, "I can't make any specific suggestions. But let me tell you this: your worth as a person doesn't depend upon your husband's evaluation of you."

There is great freedom in realizing that your personal worth doesn't depend on someone else's estimation of you. You are a person of infinite worth. Obviously, it wasn't Shakespeare who said, "I am important because God don't make no junk." But the one who did say it was right. The late Ethel Waters said, "God don't sponsor no flops." God knew what He was doing when He made you, and He didn't make a mistake. You are created in the image and likeness of God. Your value and worth do not depend upon your physical looks, athletic ability, material wealth, or intellectual capacity.

When John McKay was football coach of the University of Southern California, he was interviewed by a TV commentator. John's son was a starting end on his dad's team. The interviewer asked John to comment on the pride he felt over his son's accomplishments on the field.

"Yes, I'm pleased" he reflected, "that John had a good season last year. He does a fine job, and I am proud of him. But I would be just as proud if he had never played the game at all."

McKay appreciated his son's talent, but his worth did not depend on his ability to play football. His value was independent of his performance.[3]

God knew what He was doing when He made you. He didn't make any mistakes. In all of creation there is no one else like you. Nor until the end of time will there be another like you. A young boy who went forward in a Billy Graham Crusade told the counselor that God had made a mistake when He made him. "He should have made two Billy Grahams and not made me," he said. The counselor wisely told him, "God didn't make a mistake. If he had wanted two Billy Grahams, he would have made them. He made you for a different plan and purpose." Don't try to walk or to talk or to act like another person. God has a purpose for you.

The dodo bird lived in obscurity on three islands in the Indian Ocean until settlers came along and wiped out the defenseless birds. They looked stupid and seemed of no value. The bird looked ridiculous. Its tail was a tuft of curly feathers; its wings were stubby with no more than three or four black feathers. It had a hooked beak, large legs, and heavy feet. Its meat was fatty and lumpy, and the more they cooked it, the tougher and more untasty it became. This disgusting bird seemed worthless. But then came a surprising development. In 1977, it was discovered that the beautiful calvaria tree which grows on these islands was dependent on the dodo birds for its survival. The tree's seeds have such thick hulls that they could sprout only after going through the grinding of the dodos' digestive systems. The stupid-looking dodos served as a valuable link in the balance of nature on those obscure islands.[4]

You may not think you look like much or are of much value, but the whole picture is not seen. Everyone is important. God doesn't make worthless people. He has a definite purpose for you, even if you can't see it.

You are valuable in and of yourself. A chrysanthemum doesn't have to be a rose in order to be beautiful. It is beautiful in its own right. You are of infinite value just because you are YOU.

Your self-image involves a basic law. Frank Pollard preached on it. He said, "How you see yourself is based on the most important person in your life. You will feel about yourself what you think the most important person in your life feels about you."[5] He was right. If you make the most important person in your life someone whom you think doubts you, then you will doubt yourself. If the most important person in your life loves and believes in you, and you know it, then you will have a good image of yourself.

If you make God the most important One in your life, then you can feel good about yourself because God loves you. The Bible says, "For God so loved [you], that he gave his only begotten Son" (John 3:16). If you were the only person in this world, He would have sent Jesus Christ His Son to die on the cross just for you. And that is exactly what He did! If you have that kind of worth in the sight of God, do you have any right to think any less of yourself than God thinks of you?

So stand tall! Hold your shoulders back! Think highly of yourself! You are of infinite worth!

Accept Yourself

Next, work at accepting yourself. Our society places a high premium on physical beauty. Pretty children get more attention and encouraging strokes. Beautiful people receive preferential treatment in many situations throughout life. But unfortunately, few are blessed with outstanding good looks.

If only I didn't have so many freckles, if only my feet weren't so big, if only my mouth weren't so big, if only my knees weren't so funny looking—on and on the list could go. Teenagers, in particular, have problems accepting themselves—especially if they think someone else is better looking.

Appointment after appointment, people came all day long to view their church directory pictures. Dana, the photographer, had four or five different poses from which they could select the one for the directory and purchase any pictures they desired. The first reaction to the family pictures was the same, almost without exception: "It's good of everybody except me!" Dana, in her jovial way, would chuckle, "No one ever likes the picture of himself!" Our low self-image causes us to dislike a candid personal picture. We see some minor defect as being glaring.

Self-acceptance is so terribly important. It can deeply affect your personality. Failure to measure up can cause feelings of inferiority. It may make you tense around your peers. Some become timid and shy and may even stutter. It can cast a shadow over your entire life.

So you have to work at accepting your physical appearance.

Until you learn to accept yourself, you will always have serious inner conflicts. To free your spirit, you must learn to accept yourself as you are. Here are some ways you can work on that.

1. *Remember, physical beauty isn't everything.* It's important, but not nearly as important as inner beauty. Outward deficiencies can be overcome by developing a warm, friendly personality. You can work at being nice, polite, and friendly. The old saying, "Pretty is as pretty does," is still accurate. No matter how beautiful your face and body may be, if you don't act and talk nice, a good impression is soon destroyed. The opposite is also true. If you act right and present yourself well, outward deficiencies will seem unimportant. Others will see you as a total personality and may not even notice your scar, birthmark, or big ears.

2. *Make the best of what you have, and improve on it if you can.* If your teeth are an embarrassment for you, get braces; put porcelain caps on dark teeth, and the like. Dental work is expensive, but it is a small investment compared to how much attractive teeth add to your personal appearance. If you wear glasses, get becoming ones to your face or wear contacts. Keep yourself clean and neat. Even the poorest of folks can keep themselves clean and fresh. If you are heavy, work at losing weight and keeping it off. You will feel so much better about yourself. In short, make the best of what you have, and improve on it if you can.

3. *Wear clothes that are becoming to you.* They don't have to be expensive, but you should wear clothes that highlight your strengths and camouflage your weaknesses. People judge you by your appearance. "That's unfair," you say. True, but that's the way it is. Taking pride in your dress and appearance can give you more self-confidence. You feel better about yourself when you look better in the mirror. Your appearance affects your self-confidence. So, look your best!

4. *Develop your intellect and talents to compensate for lack*

of beauty (if that's your situation). You can't help not being beautiful, but you can study and improve your mind. Go back to school. Learn a trade. Work on a degree. Read, read, read. Others will notice your mental alertness and will be impressed. Develop your skills in playing the piano or guitar, play a sport, take up a hobby. You will feel better about yourself when you can do something special or are an expert on some topic.

I suppose we'd all like to be beautiful, but we can't all be. But you (anyone) can become a lovely and interesting person. Self-acceptance of how you look is not easy, but it is essential to improving your self-image.

Believe in Yourself

Also, you must believe in yourself. You may be your own worst enemy. Don't sell yourself short. You have more abilities and can accomplish more than you ever imagined. You can do anything you really want to do.

William James, the father of modern psychology, said in his essay, "The Energies of Man": "Men habitually use only a small part of the powers they possess, of the powers they might use." Then, he went on to say, "They use only 20 percent of their potential physically, mentally, and intellectually. Most of us operate at a 20 percent level."[6]

With God's help you can have the ability to do many of the things you really want to do. The apostle Paul captured this spirit when he said, "I can do all things through Christ which strengtheneth me" (Phil. 4:13).

In my junior year I went to Mississippi College. Previously, in junior college I had really struggled with Spanish. I finally dropped it. At college I decided to major in history and minor in secondary education. So I signed up for two history courses, a political science course, an education class, and a personal health course—all of which were needed for my degree and were required for graduation. To fulfill the two years of foreign language requirement for a Bachelor of Arts degree, I reluctantly signed up for Greek. On the first day of class, I wrote inside the cover of my textbook "I can do all things through Christ which strengtheneth me." I made it my motto for attacking Greek, plus the heavy academic load I was carrying. And I kept up my grades in all the subjects and made an *A* in Greek!

You must believe in yourself! Selma Glasser, a Brooklyn housewife, has won everything from her freezer—a car, trips to Rome, Paris, and the Caribbean—to a date with Sid Caeser and Englebert Humperdinck. How did she do it? By entering essay contests. Here's her secret. "It's 99 perfect enthusiasm," she says. "You have to say to yourself, why can't I do it as well as anybody?"[7] Selma is right. You, too, can do as well as anybody else. Don't hesitate to try. It will surprise you what all you can do.

Don't back off from big challenges. You have "what it takes"! Woody Hayes became a nationally known figure at the helm of the Ohio State Buckeyes football team. Before his long career at Ohio State, he had been coaching at the much smaller Denison and Miami universities in Ohio. "The first time I stood in the middle of the OSU stadium with its 86,000 seats staring down at me," he recalled, "I was shook up. My young son was with me, and he had hold of my hand. He must have felt my reaction for he said, 'But, Daddy, the football field is the same size.'"[8]

Stand up to a challenge. You have "what it takes"! Believe in yourself!

Maximize Your Strengths

Another way to improve your self-image is to maximize your strengths. The story is told of the animals starting a school. Each animal had to take every course in the curriculum. Of course, the rabbit could outrun all the others in the class, but he nearly killed himself trying to learn to swim.

The duck was at the head of the class in swimming, but she nearly wore off her web feet trying to learn to run. The squirrel could scamper up the tree, but he could not get off the ground in flying class.

The eagle failed all the other courses in school, but there was none in the class that could soar as high as he.

The moral of the story is that we are not all equal in ability in every area. You don't have to be good in everything.

One time I tried to sing in the church choir. I can't carry a tune! I was miserable, and I am sure I was making everybody else miserable, too. After a while I dropped out. When I realized I didn't have to be good in everything—specifically singing—I was relieved, and so was the director!

You will gain a sense of freedom when you realize you don't have to do everything well. You should not expect of yourself what you see your brothers, sisters, or friends doing. You are a unique creation of God with your own talents and abilities (Gen. 1:27).

I can't spell very well. Jokingly, I say I can't spell my name twice the same way. Neither are pronunciations and grammar my long suits. I know these are important, especially for me as a writer and a speaker. And I am constantly working to improve in these areas. However, when I realized everybody has different abilities, I didn't feel dumb anymore. This gave me a sense of freedom. I don't have to be good in every area. I'll let someone else (my secretary) spell the tricky words, pronounce the proper names, and say it grammatically correct. My strengths are in different areas.

You can do some things well and others not so well. You don't have to imitate anyone else. You don't have to engage in destructive competition. You can just enjoy being yourself. Nothing will so liberate you as taking your talents seriously. It will give you the self-confidence to be happy about the gifts of others.

We are like the animals in the story, at least to the extent that each one has limitations. No one can do everything, learn everything, or achieve everything. However, we can arrange our life so as to bring out our strong characteristics. This is not to deny the fact of our limitations. To keep from demoralizing your self-image, minimize your areas of weakness rather than keeping them in focus.

You can enhance your self-image by maximizing your strengths. To identify your God-given strengths ask yourself: "What do I like to do? What do I do well? What do others often ask me to do? What areas have I previously had successes in?"

When you have identified your strengths, arrange your life to bring out those areas of your ability. Then you will be more productive and happier doing the things that you do well.

Make Yourself Useful

Also, you should make yourself useful. Do nothing, and you will feel worthless. Everybody wants significance. You gain significance by feeling important to someone in some way. Get up and do something! Help someone! It will give you a feeling of accomplishment.

Douglas Naugler saw his life as a monotonous routine. He explained, "At work, all I had to do was to perform tasks that had long ago become automatic. At home, there were no more leaky faucets to fix, no rooms to paint. The kids were visiting relatives for the summer."

His wife sensed he felt of no use to anyone. One evening while studying she looked up from her book and noted, "When you were teaching our son to swim, you told him to keep moving, or he'd sink. Maybe it's time you took your own advice."

For a moment he stared at her. Then, he reasoned, "Of course! My life is dull because I let it be that way!" Asking God's help the next day he started moving.

His first project was the messy backyard. He turned it into a useful garden with rows of vegetables and strawberries. He swells with pride telling about it. Indoors, he moves, too. Sometimes he fills the house with the honey smell of bread baking. He hasn't stopped with projects. He involves himself in doing for others in community projects. He has taken his own advice. He just keeps moving. And now when the alarm clock goes off in the morning he praises God for giving him another day. Furthermore, Douglas Naugler reflects, "There is so much to do in God's world that we don't have to feel bored or useless."[9]

I watch TV to unwind from the intense work of preparing and preaching sermons and working with people. But if I watch too much television, I soon begin to feel like I am accomplishing nothing. It isn't long until I am upset with myself for wasting my time and mental energy on nothing worthwhile. I feel better about myself if I turn the TV off and read, help out around the house, or do something constructive.

Do nothing, and you will feel terrible. Don't just sit around. Get up, and start a project. Clean out a closet. Refinish a chair. Hoe in the garden. Volunteer as a firemen, a teacher's aid, or as a helper in a nursing home. Coach a team. Teach a class. The possibilities are limitless. Be a doer, and you will feel useful.

Don't Impose Unrealistic Expectations on Yourself

When you expect too much of yourself, and you can't deliver, feelings of inadequacy are sure to set in. Identify and reject unrealistic self-expectations.

You can't excel in every area. You can't win everything. No one can climb every mountain. Look honestly at your ability, and set realistic goals.

A friend of mine in college felt "called to preach." He was gifted as a singer, but when he tried to speak, he stuttered very badly. It was agonizing to hear him. He just couldn't get the words out. His listeners would anticipate what he was trying to say and would want to help him. It was an unrealistic expectation for him to try to preach unless God saw fit to help him overcome his stuttering. As long as I knew him, he still stuttered, and it hurt his self-image. Perhaps it would have been far better for him to give up the ambition to preach and to concentrate on his singing.

Don't constantly try to do things that are unrealistic for you. True, "Spud" Webb is playing ball in the NBA at 5′7″, but he is one in a million. And Stephen Baccus earned his law degree from the University of Miami Law School at age sixteen, but he, too, is the exception.[10] It is an unrealistic expectation for most 5′7″ people to play pro basketball or for anyone but a mental genius to earn a law degree by age sixteen.

Don't impose unrealistic expectations on yourself. To do so is to constantly butt your head against a brick wall. Concentrate your efforts in areas where you can achieve. As you reach realistic goals in life, you will feel good about yourself.

Getting It All Together

A solid sense of self-worth is not something you can take or leave. It's not a luxury. It's something you need.

No one can grow up in our pressure-cooker society with a completely wholesome self-image. It's impossible. So much value is placed on physical beauty, athletic prowess, wealth, and social standing. Children are often very cruel to one another. Youth and adults can be cutting, too. If one or a landslide of blows has caused you to have low self-esteem, you don't have to go through life with that handicap. You can change how you feel about yourself. Don't keep a poor self-image. To improve it you should:

1. *Recognize your infinite worth.* Your personal worth doesn't depend on somebody's else's estimation of you. Nor does your value depend on your performance. You are of inesti-

mable value simply because you are a choice creation. God made you in His own image and likeness. You are valuable in and of yourself.

2. *Accept yourself.* Physical beauty is not everything. It's important but not nearly as important as inner beauty. Make the best of what you have. "Pretty is as pretty does!" Developing your intellect and talents will increase your self-esteem and make you more interesting.

3. *Believe in yourself.* Don't sell yourself short. Don't back up from a challenge! You have more abilities and can accomplish more than you ever imagined.

4. *Maximize your strengths.* You can do some things well and others not so well. Don't demoralize yourself by continually trying to do what you can't do very well. Identify your areas of strength and work in those areas. You will enjoy doing what you do well and accomplish more.

5. *Make yourself useful.* Do nothing, and you will feel worthless. It is the doers who accomplish things. And the folks who accomplish things develop a good self-image.

6. *Don't impose unrealistic expectations on yourself.* Look honestly at your ability and set realistic goals. Trying to do things which are physically and intellectually beyond your ability will constantly frustrate you. Concentrate your efforts in areas where you can achieve.

A good self-image is terribly important. It doesn't guarantee happiness, but it surely plays a strategic part.

2.

Between Lunch and Breaks
A Fulfilling Work

Do you only live for quittin' time and payday? Do you re-gard work as a drudgery you have to endure to make a living?

Somewhere along the line, work has picked up a bad name. Some people pride themselves in goofing off on the job as much as possible. They think you are crazy to knock yourself out trying to do it better. They look at you like you've been standing in the sun too long if you volunteer for an additional job. They may even wonder if something is wrong with you if you really get serious about your work.

I firmly believe work is not a curse but one of life's greatest blessings. God intended for us to work. He put Adam in the Garden of Eden to dress it and to keep it (Gen. 2:15).

Work is not a curse. But lack of work is! If you don't believe it, just ask a man who is laid off what he likes best—working or lying around the house? Part of the punishment in a peniten-tiary is idleness. A work assignment is a privilege for good behavior. Some of the darkest days in this nation's history oc-curred during the Great Depression when men could not find work.

Work is not a punishment required to make a living. Instead, work is one of the most meaningful aspects of life. "We realize our greatest satisfaction in life," according to Earl Nightingale, "from our work and not from our leisure activities."[1] He's right. The happiest people are those who enjoy their work and see an accomplishment from it.

We work hard on the job, so we can enjoy leisuretime and possibly take a vacation. But in reality, this is out of focus. We should consider our work the most meaningful and important part of our life. Vacations and leisure activities are only diversion from the area which should give us our greatest pleasure—our work.

The "do-as-little-as-you-can" philosophy toward life will cause you to feel miserable and worthless. Good, tiring work can help you to be happy. I suggest you consider the following ideas to develop a better attitude toward your work.

Choose the Right Work for You

Start by choosing the right work for you. In our society with so much emphasis placed on acquiring the latest gadget, gold jewelry, and designer clothes, you may feel pressure to pursue a job you really don't like. Sure, it takes money to live! But you shouldn't go into a profession or career simply because you can make lots of money. Money is important, but it isn't nearly as important as our society thinks it is.

There is a difference in living a truly successful life and in merely making money. Some define success as achieving a large bank account and being able to buy anything one wants.

Some of the most miserable folks around are those working at a job they can't stand. Working in the oil fields, factory, or office are worthy and honorable occupations. But if you aren't feeling a sense of fulfillment, it isn't right for you.

The worth of a job is not determined by how much money you make. Becoming a doctor or lawyer just because the pay is high is not enough reason to pursue either. You may make it to the top of the economic ladder only to discover that your ladder is leaning against the wrong wall!

Pursue a vocation in the area where you really feel your talents and interest lie. The financial reward of a high-paying job is not worth the waste of talent and personal satisfaction of a job you have no interest in. You should aspire not for wealth but for happiness through job satisfaction.

Work is the only thing you can do eight hours, or more, a day, day after day, week after week, month after month, year after year. You can't eat, drink, or play eight hours a day, even though you may try. So, choose wisely the right work for you.

Actor Jack Lemmon recalls the best advice he ever received. His father was a vice-president of a company that made doughnut machines and all sorts of baked goods. Jack asked him if he could borrow three hundred bucks to go to New York to take a crack at acting.

"OK," his father said, "you don't want to start in my business. You want to act."

Jack answered, "Yes, I really need to find out if I can get anywhere with it." Of course, Jack already had done summer stock and stuff.

"You love it?"

"Yes, I love it."

His father handed him the wherewithal and said, "The day I don't find romance in a loaf of bread, I'm going to quit." Jack recalls it as a marvelous line. What he was saying was that whatever you do is not as important as loving it.[2]

"What vocation should I enter?" you ask. It is one of the most important questions in your life. You will spend more time and energy in your vocation than in any other endeavor. You should seek God's will in choosing a vocation. "Wait a minute," you say, "I'm not a preacher or a missionary. They are the ones God has a special plan for." No, you are mistaken.

You may not know many celebrities. The president may not call you on the telephone or call you by your first name. Lee Iacocca and Barbara Walters may not know you, but God knows you, and He has a plan for you.

God reveals His perfect will to all who ask Him. Pray and think about your opportunities. Be sensitive, and God will lead you. He will not lead you into something you have no interest in or ability to do. Ask yourself, "What do I enjoy doing? What am I good at?" God gave you those desires and abilities. They are clues to His direction for you.

Also, look at the job market. You wouldn't want to train for a dead end or saturated area.

Don't expect to find God's total will for your entire life at the outset. All the road signs for a long trip are not on the first twenty miles of the highway. They are spaced out and placed at strategic turns. God will reveal to you His plan as you journey through life.

Feeling good about your work is essential in achieving inner satisfaction and happiness. Keep on searching until you find God's will in your vocational choice.

Set Your Sights on Challenging Aspirations

Then, set your sights on challenging aspirations. Given average intelligence, you can do almost anything you want to. I tell my two sons, Joe and Curt, "You can do anything you want. You can be anything you want to be. No goal is too high or too hard to accomplish if you are willing to work toward a desired end."

In her book, *How To Get Whatever You Want Out of Life,* Dr. Joyce Brothers tells how she and her husband Milt wanted a Cadillac more than anything else in the world. They used to sit in front of their TV every Tuesday night watching the game show: "The $64,000 Question." It was popular in the fifties.

She kept thinking about that program: "Why can't I get on

that quiz show and earn some of the wonderful money?" She knew she could do as well as most of the contestants they had watched. She figured she could at least win enough to buy a Cadillac.

The problem was how to get on the show. Hundreds and hundreds of would-be contestants applied every week. She and Milt analyzed the contestants and their fields of expertise. It didn't take long to realize they were using contestants with paradoxical hobbies. They were looking for the unusual—the shoemaker who had an encyclopedic knowledge of grand opera or the rough, tough Marine who was a gourmet cook.

Well, she was a woman and a psychologist, and she was short and blond. What she needed was a paradoxical hobby. But what? She went through the Yellow Pages trying to find an unusual interest. Finally,. she narrowed her choices to plumbing and boxing. Milt advised her to choose boxing.

So she set to work. She viewed series of films on the great fights of the century, studied sports magazines and a book on boxing statistics. When she felt confident enough to apply, she sent off a letter describing herself as a psychologist and an expert on boxing. She also enclosed a snapshot—the fluffiest, blondest picture of herself she could find.

Two days later, the phone rang. It wasn't long until the producer of "The $64,000 Question" was asking, "Are you really a boxing expert? Can you come down to the studio?" She went for the interview, and in two weeks she was on the program.

She did well. She answered the questions and kept going on and on and on. She passed the goal she had originally set for herself—the Cadillac. And then, one night she won it all. She won *The Sixty-Four Thousand Dollars!*[3]

Be willing to take on a challenge. The story is told of a big hunter, strong and stout, who had an illustrious career. A little fellow came up to the hunter and said, "If I was as big and strong and husky as you, I'd go into the woods, and I'd kill the biggest bear I could find." The hunter responded, "Well, you know, there are some little bears in the woods, too."

If you live conservatively for fear of failure, you may end up like the lady on whose tombstone was written the words:

> Here lies the bones of Nancy Jones,
> For her, life held no terrors.
> She lived an old maid,
> She died an old maid,
> No hits, no runs, no errors!

Like Dr. Joyce Brothers, you can do almost anything you really want to do. Here's how:

First, state what you want to accomplish in the form of a goal. Write it down on paper. Express it in the form of the results you desire and set a date beside it to complete it. Until you make what you want to accomplish in the form of a goal, it is no more than a vague desire.

More than likely what you want to accomplish will make such a vast goal it will overwhelm you. So divide it into smaller goals. Make each one identifiable and tangible. That way you can see, feel, and know where you are going. With a clear direction and tangible project to complete, you can face the work of each day with enthusiasm and energy.

Second, roll up your sleeves and get to work. There are no elevators to success. You must take the stairs one step at a time. I wish I could wave a magic wand over you to make you successful. Unfortunately, there is no such wand. It isn't easy to accomplish new and difficult things. If it were, everybody would be doing it. One wise man observed, "Heights by great men reached and kept were not attained by sudden flight, but they, while their companions slept, were toiling upward in the night."[4] Success comes from perspiration more than inspiration. Triumph is just umph added to try. Only the dictionary puts "success" before "work." Dreams that are not pursued diligently are no more than daydreams. Any worthwhile achievement is always preceded by hard work.

Third, don't let discouragement defeat you. Babe Ruth struck out 1,380 times. Each time he had to determine anew to hit the ball the next time. And he did. His career home-run record of 714 stood until it was broken by Hank Aaron. Failure is never final until you quit trying. Don't give up. When you stumble, get up and try again. Figure out another way of approaching it. Remove the words *I can't* from your vocabulary.

"Hang in there! Keep on keeping on!" While sitting on a plane beside Wrigley, a friend asked the chewing gum magnate why he continued to advertise so extensively when his business was already so successful. The astute businessman responded, "For the same reason the pilot of this airplane keeps the engines running when we are already in the air."[5] We must "keep on keeping on" even when we seem to have it made.

Fourth, draw upon the resources of God. Positive thinking is not enough. God's power is available to you. "If ye have faith," Jesus said, "as a grain of mustard seed, ye shall say unto this mountain, Remove hence to yonder place; and it shall remove; and nothing shall be impossible unto you" (Matt. 17:20*b*). If you focus your faith, even if it is small, you can remove a mountain of difficulties and accomplish even the hardest tasks.

Do Your Very Best Work

Next, do your very best work. Be conscientious in your work. Do the very best you can. A large percentage of folk are only working for a paycheck. They can't wait until the weekend or vacation time comes. They take as many sick days as possible whether they are sick or not. "Only suckers work," they say. Is this your attitude?

In his book *Why Not the Best?* former President Jimmy Carter tells the story that led to the title. He had applied for the nuclear submarine program, and Admiral Rickover was interviewing him for the job. After more than two hours of discussion of various subjects, Rickover asked, "How did you stand in your class at the Naval Academy?" Filled with pride Carter responded, "Sir, I stood fifty-ninth in a class of 820!" He waited for the congratulations that never came. Instead, came the question: "Did you do your best?" The admiral asked a final question which Carter was never able to forget or to answer: "Why not?"[6]

Do you do your best in your work? If not, why not? You may rationalize, "Why should I knock myself out? After all, no one else does!" Just remember, you are not responsible for anyone but yourself. What the others do is their business and responsibility. Just do the best you can.

Our nation is filled with waiters who will not serve, carpenters who will come around someday, service station attendants who only take your money, and executives whose minds are out on the golf course. They are not trying to give better service or make a better product. They are trying to get by with doing as little as they can. These attitudes and practices are destroying America.

Put forth the extra effort to do a good job. Work hard. Do a little more than is expected of you, and you will rise to the top.

Carl Holmes tells the story of a retired business executive who was once asked the secret of his success. He replied that it could be summed up in three words: "and then some." "I discovered at an early age," he declared, "that most of the difference between average people and top people could be explained in three words. The top people did what was expected of them—and then some.

"They were thoughtful of others; they were considerate and kind—and then some. They met their obligations and responsibilities fairly and squarely—and then some. They were good friends and helpful neighbors—and then some. They could be counted on in an emergency—and then some."

I am thankful for people like that because they make the world more livable. Their spirit of service is summed up in the three little words: "and then some."[7]

By putting out your best effort, you can take pride in your work. You will feel satisfied knowing you've done your best work.

Use Your Time Wisely

Also, you should use your time wisely. "The only time that is saved is the time that is used wisely" is an old and true adage. To get your work done, you must use your time wisely. It can never be recalled. I wish I could say I use my time wisely. But I struggle with this like many of you do.

The key to using your time wisely is self-discipline. There is always time to do what you must do and usually enough time to do some of the things you want to do. Here are a few suggestions on how to get more done.

1. *Don't procrastinate.* Procrastination is putting off until tomorrow what should be done today. Don't let things drift. Get started. Begin today that project you have always dreamed about. Today is the tomorrow you have been waiting for.

Jump on it, even if it seems impossible. You may feel like the boy looking at a five-acre lawn when his daddy said, "Mow it, Son," and he had an eighteen-inch lawn mower. "I can't do it," he pleaded. "Yes, you can," his father exclaimed, "just do it one swath at a time." It took a lot of effort, but after a while the little fellow had mowed the five acres of lawn.

That's the only way you can do big tasks: a swath at a time. You cannot do all of it at one time. But you can break it down into years, then into months, and break the months into weeks. And one week at a time, you can do it. So, don't procrastinate! Break the big project into smaller units, and do it one swath at a time. Then, stay with the task. Don't bail out. Buckle down. If you work as hard at doing the job as we often do trying to get out of it, you will whittle the job down to a manageable size.

If you use the energy you expend procrastinating and worrying, and instead apply it to the job at hand, you will get it done with time left over. A successful person is "one who does what he has to do at the time he hates to do it most."[8]

2. *Do the most important things first.* Learn to do one thing, and only one thing, at a time. Do not start half a dozen jobs. Finish one project, then move on to another one.

One day an efficiency expert named Ivy Lee talked to Charles Schwab, president of Bethlehem Steel Company, trying to sell his organization's services.

Schwab responded, "What we need is not more 'knowing' but more 'doing.' If you can give us something to pep us up to do the things we already know we ought to do, I'll gladly listen to you and pay you anything you ask!"

Taking the challenge, Lee handed Mr. Schwab a blank note sheet and instructed, "Write on this paper the six most important tasks you have to do tomorrow." Schwab proceeded. "Now," said Lee, "number them in the order of their importance." When Schwab finished, Lee continued, "Now, put this paper in your pocket and the first thing tomorrow morning look at item one and start working on it until it is finished. Then tackle item two in the same way, then item three, and so on. Do this until quitting time. Don't be concerned if you have only finished one or two. You'll be working on the most important ones. The others can wait. If you can't finish them all by this method, you couldn't have with any other method either.

"Do this every working day. After you've convinced yourself of the worth of this system, have your men try it. Try it as long as you wish, and then send me a check for what you think it is worth."

In a few weeks Schwab sent Lee a check for $25,000 with a letter saying the lesson on management was the most profitable one he had ever learned.[9]

Every Sunday night, Chrysler Chairman Lee Iacocca gets the adrenaline going by making a list of what he wants to accomplish during the coming week. Using this method, he is able to get his work done and keep the weekends free for family and recreation.

After observing others he remarked, "I'm amazed by the number of people who can't seem to control their own schedules. Over the years, many executives have said to me with pride: 'Boy, I worked so hard last year that I didn't take any vacation.' I always feel like responding: 'You dummy. You mean to tell me that you can take responsibility for an eighty-million-dollar project and you can't plan two weeks out of the year to have some fun?'"[10]

3. *Don't over-obligate yourself.* Consider carefully the work involved in an additional job before taking it on. Ask, "Is this really what I want to do? Am I willing to put forth the effort to do a good job?" It is better to do a few things well than to attempt too much and only do it halfway. Realizing you don't have to do everything is a great liberation.

Don't let trivial things devour your time. A busy housewife, writer, and teacher was asked, "How do you have time to do everything?" "That's easy," she replied, "I don't do everything. I just do first what I think is most important."

Use your time wisely. You will accomplish more and be happier when you do.

Don't Work Seven Days a Week

Last, but not least, don't work seven days a week. Refuse to drive yourself seven days a week! You can get so caught up in the hassle of making a living you do not take time to really live.

For your physical and mental well-being, God asked you to set aside one day out of every seven for rest, relaxation, and worship. "Remember the sabbath day, to keep it holy. Six days shalt thou labour, and do all thy work: But the seventh day is the

sabbath of the Lord thy God: in it thou shalt not do any work"
(Ex. 20:8-10*a*). God gave you the sabbath (for most
Christians—Sunday, the Lord's Day) as a reward for your labor. After your labor you deserve to rest. If you don't rest on
the sabbath you are only cheating yourself.

One day out of every seven, you need to stop your regular
schedule of work and get some rest. The relaxation will recharge and renew your body. Gerald Kennedy told this story
from the gold rush days. Two parties started out traveling
across the plains, going west to California. One was led by a
religious man, and they stopped each Lord's day for worship
and rest. The other group was led by an irreligious man who
was so anxious to reach the gold of California that he would not
take time to stop. He drove his group every day. An amazing
thing happened. The party that stopped on Sunday arrived
first.[11]

I believe you can get just as much done and probably more by
not working on Sunday. Stopping for worship and rest each
Sunday will not hurt your productivity. To the contrary, in the
long run I think it will help it.

You can be just as good a student in college if you don't
study on Sunday. The farmer can get his crop planted and har-
vested six days a week as well as the fellow who tries to work
seven days a week. The same applies to storekeepers and sales-
people. You will have to be more careful about working and
using your time wisely the other six days. But if you will, you
will get your job done without burning yourself out over the
long haul.

During my college days I started taking a Sunday afternoon
nap and tried not to study on Sunday unless I really was in a
tight. I made it just fine, and the last two years I made some of
the best grades and carried a bigger and harder school load than
any other time during my life. I am still enjoying the Sunday
afternoon nap. It does more to recharge my body and mind than

anything I do all week. It is a "must" for me. Take time to rest on your day of worship. You deserve it. You have earned it! Vance Havner noted, "Unless we come apart and rest awhile, we may just plain come apart."[12] Slow down to catch up!

Also, we need to recreate our souls. A group of explorers who went to Africa employed some native guides. They began their journey in a rush and continued to do so on the second, third, and consecutive days. On the seventh day, they noticed the guides sitting under a tree. "Come on," they barked. "We no go today," replied the guides. "We rest today to let our souls catch with our bodies."[13]

God gave us the sabbath to recharge our spirits. So take time each week to worship in a church of your choice. The inspiring music and prayers will lift your soul and give you hope. Regular worship will help you survive the strain and anxiety of daily life. It will help you keep a clear view of God and His high purpose for your life.

During my school days we would say, "TGIF" (Thank Goodness, It's Friday!), with an air of relief. Frank Pollard, speaker of "At Home with the Bible," has penned the letters *PGIS* (Praise God, It's Sunday).

Getting It All Together

All my life I've heard, "Hard work never hurt anybody." It's true. Sure, it makes you tired. It's the lack of enough to do that causes anxiety and misery, not hard work. Roll up your sleeves, and go to work. To enjoy your work more:

1. *Choose the right work for you*. Some of the most miserable folks around are those working at jobs they can't stand. So choose wisely. Pursue a vocation where you really feel your talents and life can count. Seek God's will in choosing the right work for you.

2. *Set your sights on challenging aspirations*. Be willing to take on a challenge. You can do almost anything you really

want to do. To achieve challenging aspirations, you must state what you want to accomplish in the form of a goal. Work hard to achieve it. Avoid letting discouragement defeat you, and draw deeply upon the resources of God.

3. *Do your very best work*. Put forth the best effort you can. Take pride in your work. Do more than is required. Work harder than is expected, and you will feel personal satisfaction knowing you have done your best.

4. *Use your time wisely*. Self-discipline is the key. Don't procrastinate! Begin today. There's no better time than the present to get started. Learn to do the most important things first. And be careful not to over-obligate yourself.

5. *Don't work seven days a week*. God intended for you to rest on the sabbath. He gave it to us as a reward for working. You need it to recharge your body and mind. You can accomplish as much in six days as seven when you take a day a week to rest. Also take time each week to worship in a church of your choice. It will renew your spirit.

The hardworking people I know are the happiest. The people who don't have enough to do are bored and miserable. So consider work a high privilege, not a punishment required to make a living.

Don't be afraid to work hard; your greatest happiness is found in it. "If God simply handed us everything we wanted, He'd be taking from us our greatest prize—the joy of accomplishment."[14]

3.

All I Have to Offer You Is Me
A Generous Spirit

"Tell Santa what you want for Christmas, little girl."

"Nothing for me," she said, "but I want rent money for Mommy."

When a big girl was asked what she wanted for Christmas she replied, "A Mercedes Benz convertible, a ten-room house, a million dollars, and Tom Selleck."

The requests of the little girl and the big girl contrast the attitude many have toward money. Many, like the big girl, are trying to get all they can just for themselves. Others are like the little girl. They are generous givers. She was wanting the money not for herself but to help her mother.

Where money is concerned, people can be divided into two groups—getters and givers. The getters hoard all they can. They're always after the best for themselves. The givers don't think about how much they can accumulate but how much they can share with others. Which are you: a getter or a giver?

Generous people are generally happy. Miserly people are generally unhappy about many things. Stingy people are usually critical or mad about something.

For a life filled with joy and purpose, learn to be a giver, not a getter. Jesus was right when He said, "It is more blessed to give than to receive" (Acts 20:35*b*). Do you believe that? The one who gives receives a greater blessing than the one who receives. Let's count the ways.

Happiness

First, giving will make you happy. Food tastes better when you share it. You enjoy a waterfall more when you're there with someone else. The amazing feats in a circus are more enjoyable when you bring a friend along to share them with you. Christmas is more meaningful when you give to others less fortunate than yourself.

During seminary, my wife Violet and I attended a mission church that met in a revamped residential house. Mattie, a precious black woman, worked with preschoolers. Her husband and four children left for Texas to visit relatives as soon as school was out on Friday for the Christmas holidays. A few days before Christmas the Ice Follies was running nightly in San Francisco. Violet and I decided to go, and we asked Mattie to go with us. She was lonely with her husband and children gone for Christmas. Mattie hadn't seen anything that compared with the lights, costumes, music, and ice skating of the Follies. She was overwhelmed. She was like a child eating cotton candy for the first time. Our enjoyment of the Follies was multiplied. We were seeing it not as just another production, but we were seeing through the eyes and elation of Mattie. I shall never forget how much she enjoyed it and how much she appreciated our taking her. The way she enjoyed it made us enjoy it more, too. Mattie's excitement over the program and the way she enjoyed the evening made Christmas meaningful to us that year.

By giving a portion of what you have you will realize a greater happiness in life. You can help a young person go to college, warm an elderly couple's home, provide for underprivileged children, or a hundred other good things. It makes you feel so good to know you have done something worthwhile.

Your enjoyment increases as you share.

It has been said there are three kicks to money. One comes in making it, another in having it, and the third, in giving it. If you miss the third kick, you miss the best one of the three.

Greedy persons can't see beyond themselves. They want all the luxuries, land, and money they can get. They grab everything within their reach, and keep it. They think if they don't look out for themselves, they will never be happy. But the fact of the matter is: the opposite is true. Giving brings happiness.

You might think, *If only I had $100,000. Then I would share*. But, no matter what your income, instinctively you will use it all on yourself. It doesn't take great wealth to be greedy. Let me emphasize you can be just as stingy with $100 as you can with $100,000.

The trouble with money is: it tempts you to hoard. The more you get the more you want. While it is right to prepare for emergencies and retirement by saving, it is wrong to hoard. It isn't always easy to distinguish between saving and hoarding. You must examine your motives to assure savings are in proper balance with generous giving and not simply to amass wealth.

Money is important. But it is not synonymous with happiness. Dr. Joyce Brothers observed, "Money can buy happiness, *but only up to a point*."

Perhaps people who make $30,000 a year are happier than those with only a $10,000 income. But most individuals will be no happier with $150,000 than with $30,000. Yes, they can dress better, own a fancier car, and vacation in more exotic places, but they will not be significantly happier.

Dr. Brothers explained: you are miserable if you're cold and hungry and unable to buy shoes for your children. And you're happy when you find a job or get a raise, so you can buy warmth and food and give your children the things they need. But as soon as your income reaches the point where you have enough money to provide for the necessities and some left over for pleasures, any additional money can only add little more to your happiness.[1]

Hoarding an abundance of money won't make you any happier. But sharing that abundance will bring you a certain amount of happiness.

Satisfaction

Second, giving will bring you satisfaction. "Let us put your money to work" is the theme of many bank commercials. It points out the advantages of putting your money to work in their bank. The same is true of love. For love to do any good, it too has to be put to work. Improve your investment program. Put your love to work by giving unselfishly to help others.

Maybe you can't give your nights and days to underprivileged children and the mentally retarded, but by giving to the United Way you can attend them. Maybe you can't go with healing in your fingers to the heart of Africa to tend the bodies of the people there, but by your giving you can stand by missionaries who do. You can't devote all your time and energies to ministering to the sick, distressed, and spiritually empty, but by your church offerings you can provide for those who are called to do so. You may not be able to do it yourself, but you can make it possible. You can underwrite the work of others with your money. Putting your love to work by giving unselfishly to help others is an investment that produces dividends of abiding satisfaction.

Money has no value except in its use. Benjamin Franklin once wrote: "The use of money is all the advantage there is in having money."[2] Giving to help others is a wise investment. I don't know anyone who doesn't want to make a good investment.

A certain amount of joy is found in living moderately, so you can help others. Seemingly, many don't think so. They are always on a quest for something newer and better. After getting a television, they have to have a video game. It isn't long until they want a VCR. But, then, they realize the movies would look better on a wide-screened set. And all of this would be easier to operate with a remote control. The list is endless. One cannot find satisfaction in acquiring more and more things. The more we have, the more we want. It is an unending quest.

The Romans had a proverb which said that money was like sea water: the more a man drinks, the thirstier he becomes. As long as we only think about our money and our wants, we will never be satisfied.

John Wesley's rule of life was to "save" all he could and "give" all he could. When he was at Oxford, he had an income of 30 pounds a year. He lived on 28 pounds and gave away two pounds. When his income increased to 60 pounds, and then 120 pounds a year, he still lived on 28 pounds and gave the balance away.

The accountant-general for Household Plate of England demanded a return from Wesley. His reply was, "I have two silver tea spoons at London and two at Bristol. This is all the plate which I have at present; and I shall not buy any more, while so many around me want bread."[3] Instead of aggressively buying everything you want, deny yourself and give some away.

It is more satisfying to help someone else than to indulge in selfish luxuries. Giving will help you to be more satisfied with what you have rather than longing for what you don't have.

Satisfaction is not a matter of material possessions but an attitude to be learned. Frank Pollard was filling in the blanks of a questionnaire and was confronted by this inquiry: "Are you independently wealthy?" He reasoned with himself, "Well, I know I'm kind of independent at times, and I've always believed that anyone who has plumbing in his house and food on the table is wealthy." So he wrote, "yes"![4] Wealth is a state of mind, not bank accounts or possessions.

More isn't necessarily better! A tour group observed an old

historic farm in the bluegrass area of Kentucky. As the bus rolled past the genteel farm that had been there for years, someone spoke up, "That is such a beautiful place. Surely the people that live on that farm with all those beautiful horses must be very, very happy." The tour conductor said, "Oh, I am sorry to tell you that is not so. That house has had in it three generations, and all three generations have had nothing but sorrow, tragedy, and heartbreak.

"The first generation—the woman committed suicide, and it left such a shadow over that house that some said it was haunted. The second generation—the man was an alcoholic. He died an early death and left a widow who mismanaged the farm, and it went down. The third generation—it fell into the hands of quarreling children, and the estate is now in litigation as the children fight over possession of it and hate each other."[5] More is not always better. True riches are not in possessions but in enjoying what you have.

Confidence

Third, giving will make you more confident. How? By being a giver you have to trust God to take care of your needs.

He will not let you down. He is able to meet your needs. The apostle Paul told the generous Philippians, "My God shall supply all your need according to his riches in glory by Christ Jesus" (4:19).

God is big enough and willing to take care of you if you trust Him to do so. "The earth is the Lord's, and the fulness thereof; the world, and they that dwell therein" (Ps. 24:1). "For every beast of the forest is mine, and the cattle upon a thousand hills," says the Lord in Psalm 50:10. God owns everything, and His power is unlimited.

Your giving prompts God to give to you. God is generous, and He loves to bless generous people.

Giving should not stop with just sharing with others. The

Bible teaches you are to give back to God a portion of what He has given you.

In earlier years, there was a group of hard-working farmers known as sharecroppers. They worked on the land owned by another. For the use of the land and equipment, they shared the harvest with the owner. In a sense, we are sharecroppers on God's land. We are to return a tithe of our income to Him as a reminder that God is indeed the Owner of all things. It is all too easy to see ourselves seated at the center of the universe.

A church outgrew its building and needed to build. The city building code, however, contained a regulation that would force the church to provide more parking space if the building were to be enlarged. The church didn't own enough land to expand both building and parking space. A supermarket, which was closed on Sundays, had a parking lot adjoining the church property. The city planning commission determined that if the church could negotiate a contract to use that parking lot, the church could also build the needed expansion. A meeting was arranged to formalize a contract that would satisfy the church, the supermarket manager, and the city.

To the delight of the church the supermarket did not require a fee. Only one stipulation was placed in the contract. One Sunday a year, the parking lot entrances would be closed and locked, and the church members would not have access to the lot. The manager explained, "All other Sundays of the year you may use the parking lot free of charge. One Sunday a year you will not have access to the parking lot to remind you that the parking lot belongs to the supermarket and not to the church."

The Bible teaches the tithe (one tenth of your income) is God's. "Bring ye all the tithes into the storehouse, that there may be meat in mine house, and prove me now herewith, saith the Lord of hosts, if I will not open you the windows of heaven, and pour you out a blessing, that there shall not be room enough to receive it" (Mal. 3:10).

Ever since I have earned an income I have tithed. I can truth-fully say I have not and do not worry about paying our bills. Tithing has helped me to depend more upon God. I have confidence He will take care of me. If you aren't a tither, I highly recommend that you try it. You'll be glad you did.

A man in a Midwestern state used a unique method to encourage Christians to tithe. He was often heard to say, "I'm so convinced tithing is right that I challenge you just to try it for three months. If it has not brought you spiritual satisfaction and joy, then I'll pay you the difference between your tithe and the offering you would have given." A number of people accepted his challenge and began to tithe. He never had a person report that it had not been a spiritually rewarding experience. To the best of his knowledge, those who accepted his challenge never abandoned their new giving practice. For many, it seemed to be linked to a period of spiritual growth.[6] It gave them new confidence in God's ability to help them meet their needs.

You can't outgive God! The story is told of a dedicated farmer who loved the Lord and tithed. His friends asked him how he gave so much and yet remained so prosperous. "We can't understand," they said, "how you can give more than the rest of us, and yet you always seem to have greater prosperity." "Oh," answered the farmer, "that is very easy to explain. You see, I keep shoveling into God's bin, and God keeps shoveling into mine, and He has the bigger shovel."

Giving will make you more dependent upon God. By depending upon Him you can face each day with confidence. You can trust Him to help you meet your needs.

Spiritually

Fourth, giving will help you to grow spiritually. Giving through your church will help you to become more interested in spiritual matters. Jesus taught, "Lay not up for yourselves treasures upon earth, where moth and rust doth corrupt, and where

thieves break through and steal: But lay up for yourselves treasures in heaven . . . For where your treasure is, there will be
your heart be also'' (Matt. 6:19-21). Whatever you put your
money into, you will be interested in.

For years you may have passed a certain corner on your way
to work without ever really noticing the office buildings and
parking lot there. Suppose it came up for sale, and you bought
it for $100,000. Your interest in that same corner would in-
crease considerably because now you have sunk part of your
life's savings into it. Each time you pass, you'll push in on the
brake and turn your head to look it over—dreaming about how
you will upgrade it.

Earthly possessions tend to chain you to material interests.
Your treasures in life are only temporary holdings. Just about
the time a man says, ''I've got it made,'' time runs out on him.
In death, all his possessions pass into the hands of another. A
man arrogantly talks about *my* house and *my* land. In just a few
years, somebody else will be saying *my* house and *my* land, and
ironically, they will be talking about the same property!

Temporary holdings do not constitute real riches. By invest-
ing in Christ's work through His church, you will become more
interested in spiritual things. The more you give, the more you
grow spiritually.

A pastor visited a man in a small town and was talking with
him about his decision to accept Christ. They had talked many
times about this matter. The man very pointedly told the pastor,
''Preacher, I want to accept Christ. I want to join the church.
But what I do with my money is my business.''

The man made his decision for Christ, identified with the
church, and began to take an active part. He grew spiritually. It
was not long until he was a committed steward of his possessions in service to the Lord.

The preacher approached him one day and said, ''I thought
you felt what you did with your money was your business.''

The man grinned and replied, "That's right, what I do with my money is still my business. It's just that my business has changed!"

Giving to the Lord's work through His church will cause you to change your business from material holdings to spiritual ones. Your interest will follow your holdings: "For where your treasure is, there will your heart be also."

Television commercials and newspaper ads are basically telling you to consume, consume, consume, now, now, now: you deserve it. TV game shows are subtly reinforcing the same message through the excitement of people winning cars, money, furniture, trips, etc. If you are not careful you will begin to think real life consists primarily of getting things and going places to enjoy comfort and to find pleasure.

If you let your appetite go unchecked, it will grow to almost unlimited proportions. As long as you think only about your needs and wants, you will constantly desire to get bigger, newer, and shinier things.

If God has blessed you with an abundance of material success, and it hasn't entered your mind to give any of it away, you more than likely have an unchecked appetite for more and more.

Janet Dillard, a missionary homemaker in Kenya, spoke recently in our church. She, alongside her husband Jim, a high school teacher, sees severe poverty daily. They agonize that the missionaries can't do more to clothe and feed the people. She told us that many Kenyans make less than $300 a year income—less than most of us make per week. "With God's blessings," she shared, "comes a greater responsibility to share some of what we have."

We are responsible to give according to our ability. The larger our incomes and the greater the ability, the greater amount we should give. The family who has an annual income of $100,000 is responsible for giving far more than the family whose annual income is $12,000. The more God blesses us financially, the more we should give. Generous giving is not measured by the amount given but by what is kept to use on self.

How do you overcome an inordinate desire for things? Well, how did you forget the boy or girl you were madly in love with in high school? Why, you met someone else! How do you get rid of the greed that destroys your life or the covetousness that drives you to be less than you ought to be? Why, you meet Someone Who can change your desires. That Someone is Jesus.

How to Enjoy Giving

Duty is a marvelous virtue, but it can be awfully joyless. I have preached a lot of sermons on tithing both from the New Testament and the Old. The Scriptures truly teach tithing, and I can make a solid case of why Christians ought to tithe. But if we do it only because the Bible says we ought to, we are not going to enjoy it much. We may do it, but it will gall us to write out the check each week. Duty is a wonderful, wonderful thing, but there's more.

The bloated bellies and pencil-thin legs of little Ethiopian children upon the television screen is heartwrenching. In a moment you see actress Sally Struthers pleading with you to send money to help feed the poor, hungry children. You feel guilty for having so much when you see children on the screen without enough to eat. The guilt nags at your conscience. To release that terrible feeling, you pull out your checkbook and write a check for $50. In this instance, guilt was a good feeling, and it caused you to help the hungry children. When guilt causes you to do a good thing, it is positive. But there's more.

The letter has your name on it, and you quickly look to see who it's from. The return address lists your alma mater. As you open it, you realize it is another letter from the alumni president asking for your financial support for the college. You file it in File 13—the round file at the end of the desk. You forget about it until the telephone rings, and a college representative personally asks you to contribute. Being a good, upstanding graduate of the school, you don't want to seem like a heel or a cheapskate, so you pledge $10 or $20. After all, it's harder to turn down a person on the telephone than to throw away an alumni letter. You gave because of the persistent prodding and pressure. It motivated you to do a good thing: help support higher education. External pressure can cause you to give. But there's more.

To give from duty, guilt, or external pressure can do a lot of good and help many people, but there's no joy in it. What's wrong? We must learn how to enjoy giving. We must learn to give out of two inner motives. One is a deep love for other people, and the other is a genuine gratitude for God's blessings.

When our hearts are filled with love for other people, we will generously give and enjoy every bit of it. The loving person considers the needs of others instead of continually thinking about his own needs and wants. He strives to see how much he can give rather than how little. His only regret when he has given all he can is that he doesn't have more to give.

> Love ever gives,—
> Forgives—outlives,—
> And ever stands
> With open hands,
> And, while it lives,
> It gives.
> For this is Love's prerogative,—
> To give,—and give,—and give.[7]

Love will motivate us to give ourselves to help others. Missionary surgeon John Tarpley traded prestige and big money in the United States for water shortages and exhausting patient loads in Nigeria. He could be living in a prestigious house and driving a Porsche, but he has no complaints. "I get paid in different currency," he claims, "healed patients, grateful parents of recovering children, the fulfillment of training young Nigerian doctors."[8]

Genuine gratitude will cause us to enjoy giving. It will prompt giving. The parents of a young man killed in warfare gave the church a check as a memorial to their son. When the presentation was made, another war mother whispered to her husband, "Let's give the same for our boy." "What're you talking about?" he asked. "Our son didn't lose his life." "That's just the point," replied the wife, "let's give it because he was spared."

A deep sense of appreciation for what the Lord has done for us will cause us to enjoy giving. One man testified, "The thing I'm most grateful for this Thanksgiving Day is, when the Lord was deciding who would need help at this season and who would be in a position to give that help, He permitted me to be among the givers." Grateful persons give and are glad they are able to do so.

Getting It All Together

This world is made up of two kinds of people: getters and givers. The getters get all they can and "can" all they get. Their only concern is themselves. The givers aren't too concerned about how much they can accumulate but seek to share all they can.

Generous people are generally happy. Miserly people are generally unhappy. By giving generously to the Lord's work and to help others you will find:

1. *Happiness*. You enjoy what you have more when you share with others. The trouble with money is it tempts one to hoard. By giving a portion of what we have, we will realize a greater happiness in life.

2. *Satisfaction*. Putting our love to work through unselfish

giving pays handsome dividends. By giving we share in helping many people whom we wouldn't have time or energy to help otherwise. Instead of indulging in selfish luxuries, live modestly so you can help others. Giving pays such dividends of lasting satisfaction. Everyone enjoys a good investment.

3. *Confidence*. When we give, we must rely on God to help us take care of all our personal needs. To tithe, most folks have to depend upon God to help them meet their obligations. By depending upon God we can face each day with confidence. Thus, the anxiety of making ends meet is gone. Giving helps us to be more confident.

4. *Spiritually*. Our interest is in the things we put our money in. If we invest in houses, land, and cars we are interested in material matters. If we invest in Christ's work through the church, we will become more interested in spiritual things. The more we give, the more we grow spiritually. Our interest shifts from temporary holdings to spiritual things.

Giving out of a sense of duty can be awfully joyless. Guilt and external pressure can propel us to give, but they can be most painful. We need to learn how to enjoy giving. The inner motives that produce joyous giving are love and gratitude. Proper inner motives change giving from a drudgery into a joyous opportunity.

Happiness isn't a secret. The generous giver will experience a great deal of happiness. Indeed, it is more blessed to give than to receive.

4.

Thanksgiving and Thanksliving
A Grateful Heart

A grateful heart is another element of happiness. Persons who are thankful for what they have live a happier life than those who are ungrateful. The grateful person is a happy person.

In a survey of nearly 100,000 Americans, a Columbia University professor revealed that a person's happiness in regards to the influence of money and education has to do with one's original expectations. If you thought you'd earn a lot because of advanced degrees—and did—you have a "so-what?" attitude. But if your expectations are overfulfilled, the happiness that comes from getting more than you thought you would can be quite pronounced.[1] The happiest people are those who get more than they expected. The reason they are happy is because they realize something to be happy about.

Thankfulness does not so much depend on what we have. If it did, those who have the most would be the happiest. But it depends on our point of view. Thankfulness is not a question of whether or not we have a lot but whether we are thankful for what we have.

Why We're Ungrateful

Instead of being thankful for all they have, many people are ungrateful. Dr. Wayne Dehoney, former pastor of Walnut Street Baptist Church, Lousiville, gave four reasons for ingratitude in a Thanksgiving message.[2] They explain why so many are ungrateful. By better understanding the reasons for our ingratitude, we can more easily develop a thankful spirit.

Taking Life and Its Blessings for Granted

One of the basic reasons why we are ungrateful is that we simply take life and its blessings as a matter of course. An old song goes, "You don't miss the water until the well runs dry." It's true; we don't appreciate the value of things until they are gone. When everything is going fine, we accept it as a matter of fact.

As a nation we enjoy so much, it's easy to assume everyone has what we have. Since many people have a nice car, fine clothes, a well-built house, and plenty to eat, we fail to realize that others don't have it as well as we do. We forget that millions die without ever having had enough to eat, a home to go to, a bicycle to ride, or even clothes to keep them warm.

We take our health for granted. Mrs. Donia Fleming was a roommate of my great aunt at Colonial Terrace Nursing Home. She was losing the feeling in her hands due to poor blood circulation. She explained, "I never thought about how important feeling is to your hands until I started losing mine." We never stop to think how valuable our health is until we start losing it.

Being a parent, I know how it feels to be so aggravated at your kids you are ready to sell them along with the old bicycles and tools in a yard sale. When they get under foot, I start snapping orders like a drill sergeant. Amid the emotional, financial, and energy drain caused by children, it is so easy to forget how important they are and what a blessing it is to have children.

I read about a man who lived with his six children in Philadelphia. Just before school was to start, all of his children
needed new shoes. At the same time, the washing machine
played out. To top it all off, his work was reduced because of
bad weather.

He was able to manage the shoes, but he was short on cash
for a new washer. He placed an ad for a used machine in the
paper. He answered a call offering what he figured he could
afford. While picking up the washer he noticed the home was
filled with all the comforts anyone could ever want. The conversation got around to the children, and he commented on the
problems of feeding and clothing that many children. The
woman of the house ran out of the room crying. In explaining,
her husband shared that they had one child who had been para-
lyzed from birth, and therefore had never needed a pair of
shoes. When the man arrived home with the used machine, he
picked up the old shoes, worn out from skipping rope, kicking
rocks, and jumping puddles. Kneeling by his bed he thanked
God for the worn-out shoes in his house. It's so easy to take our
children's healthy bodies for granted.

When it is unseasonably warm and dry and the harvest is
progressing ahead of schedule, the farmer doesn't think much
about the weather. Then it begins to rain; then fields don't dry
up completely before it sets into raining again. With every wet
day he becomes more anxious to put the combine back into the
field to harvest his soybeans and corn. He knows if he doesn't
get the crop out soon, it will wind up on the ground and be
impossible to harvest. His stomach turns, and his nerves tense
as more clouds gather. Now he is praying, "Lord, give us some
dry days. Let the sun shine. Lord, give us good harvesting days
again, and I will be grateful!" Conversely, he is at times faced
with drought when he prays with all his being for rain.

You see, we simply take life and its blessings as a matter of course when everything is going well. Ingratitude is partially born out of taking God's blessings for granted.

Having Too Much Pride and Conceit

Another reason we are ungrateful is because of our pride and our conceit. At times we may believe that our lives are what we make them. We may feel the good things that happen are our own doing. And when we prosper, we might feel it's because we are just a little smarter than everybody else. If we stand out for an honor, we surmise it's because of who we are. When we rise to the top of a sport, a corporate ladder, or a prominent place in government, it's easy to think we're self-made.

We had better be careful about saying we prospered because of our ability, our talent, our drive, or our ingenuity. God has a way of bringing us down when we become too conceited. A certain farmer's neighbor came down to see his place. The farmer invited, "Come on in! I want you to see my new house. I've just built a new kitchen back here. Look at my new garage! How do you like my new car? Come on now and let me show you my new machinery. Let's walk around and look over my farm. I'll show you what I have done to improve my barns." His wife listened to all that was said. But after the neighbor left, she took out a frying pan and started after him. She slapped him on the side of the head and said, "It is not *yours:* it's *ours!*" She socked him on the other side of the head and said, "Remember, *ours . . . ours . . . ours!*"

He learned his lesson! About four o'clock the next morning, the alarm went off for him to get up and milk the cows before daylight. As he was fumbling around in the dark trying to find his clothes, she asked, "What's the matter with you? Why are you making so much noise?" He replied, "Honey, I can't find *our* britches."

We had better be careful about how much we feel our

achievements rest only on our own accomplishments. God can make us quickly say *our britches* at anytime.

In this materialistic age, it is so easy to think, *My business supports me and my family*. We seldom stop to realize everything we have, and everything we ever hope to have, depends upon God's help and abundant provision.

Such was the case of the boy carrying a sack when a man asked him, "What have you got there?"

"A loaf of bread," he replied.

"Where did you get it?"

"From the baker."

"Where did the baker get it?"

"He made it."

"Of what did he make it?"

"Flour."

"Where did he get the flour?"

"From the miller."

"Where did he get it?"

"From the farmer."

"Where did the farmer get it?"

Then the truth dawned upon the boy, and he replied, "From God."

"Well, then, from where did you get the loaf?"

"Oh, from God!"

In the last resort, the boy acknowledged God to be the Giver of what he possessed. Aren't we like this boy?

Also, we owe so much to others for helping us. Who can unequivocally say, "I am a self-made man"? Sir Isaac Newton wrote in a letter to Robert Hooks, "If I have seen further than you . . . it is by standing upon the shoulders of giants."[3]

Only when you turn from your pride and conceit can you ever be grateful. There are many who have worked harder and not been blessed nearly as much. The only explanation is that God has been good to you. There are numerous people as smart as you, and yet they have seen all kinds of trouble. Maybe you are farther ahead than they, and the only reason is: God has been good. You excel not because you are better than most but because of the help of God and others. No one is self-made.

Brooding Over Misfortunes

Another cause for ingratitude is brooding over the bad that happens to us. Let one bad thing happen to us, and we let it so dominate our lives that we fail to see the many good things we have enjoyed.

It is so easy to focus on the one bad thing to the exclusion of a dozen good things. Maybe you did have it hard growing up. Or you didn't have an opportunity to finish school. Or you had to work hard and never were able to have time or money enough really to enjoy yourself. But is that any reason not to see the blessings of a steady job and good friends?

Or you have gone through the heartbreak of a divorce, but is that any reason to be ungrateful for your health, a place to live, and friends at work and at church?

Yes, you have lost a child, yet you have three other children. Are you going to mourn constantly over the one you lost until you can't be happy about the three beautiful, healthy children in your home?

Certainly bad things will happen to you! They do to everybody. That doesn't mean you should overlook the good things in your life. One doesn't dig up the flowers in one's garden because of a few weeds.

Our outlook in life affects our sense of gratitude. Two men are eating grapes. One is sad because of the seeds, and the other is thankful for the fruit to eat. Two women examine a rose. One complains about the thorns, and the other enjoys the gorgeous petals and delicious scent.

You must realize that if you face the sun the shadows will fall behind you, but if you turn your back on the sun all the shadows will be in front of you. If you focus on the good, you can find plenty to be thankful for. If you focus on the bad, you can find enough to make you sad. Beware because it is easy to let the bad things dominate you until you fail to see the many good things that are yours.

Feeding on Envy and Jealousy

Another reason for ingratitude is envy and jealousy. Seeing the good things that happen to another can work on us until we despise our own blessings because they are not as great as the other person's.

The boy was proud of the new bike he received for Christmas until he discovered his best friend had gotten one with gears on it. The teenager was happy about getting a telephone extension in her room until she learned her friend had her own private line. The woman was pleased to have a job until she learned her friend was getting an easier job with higher pay.

A man was proud of his brand-new Chevrolet until he realized his neighbor had bought a new Lincoln Continental. He became so envious and resentful he ceased to be happy and could not enjoy the car he had. He wasn't satisfied until he had a car as good or better than his neighbor's.

Aren't we all guilty of looking at our circumstances and saying, "Oh, so and so has it so much better than I do. I wish I had his job"? If we are not careful, we will let envy and jealousy cause us to be dissatisfied with what we have.

Blessings Should Be Counted

A father was hurrying toward home one winter night with his little daughter at his side when suddenly she said to him, "Father, I am going to count the stars"

"Very well," he answered, "go on."

By and by he heard her counting "223, 224, 225. Oh dear," she said, "I had no idea there were so many."

He wisely replied, "My dear, the stars are just like God's blessings. There are so many of them that we can never count them all!"

Everyone has blessings to count. Have you tried to count yours recently? Just look around you. What do you see? Do you have a cozy home, warm clothes, food enough, and a job?

In times past, people frequently didn't have enough to eat. If our forefathers could sit down to a typical meal of our day, they would think they were feasting in a king's palace! Not only should we be thankful for food but for an appetite to eat. It is better to sit down to a simple meal with an appetite than to a banquet table loaded with delicacies and be unable to eat.

If your home is comfortable and cozy, it is a lot to be thankful for. I can't imagine living on the streets as literally thousands do in the major cities of our land. No matter how humble your home may be, it is still home. I always enjoy going away on vacation, but I never go any place or see anything I am more glad to see than our home when we return.

Clothes are also a blessing. Your jeans may not be Jordache, your shirts may not be IZOD, nor your tennis shoes Air Jordans, but if your clothes are warm and comfortable you have plenty to be grateful for. Perhaps you can go out and buy any clothes you need whenever you want, but not everybody can. Many have to wear hand-me-downs. Many children wear shoes that are not good for their feet because their parents can't do any better or simply don't care.

You may not like your job. It may be the pits as far as you are concerned. The pay may be less than average. But if your work gives you a regular income, be thankful. Many are just as well qualified and ambitious as you are, but they can't find work. They don't like having to depend on food stamps and odd jobs to make it. Many are getting further behind with every month that rolls by with no prospect of things changing. A steady job, even one you don't like, is something to be thankful for.

At times we may take our families for granted. Having a mate or brothers and sisters to share our hurts and joys with is a blessing. When Curt was small, he often prayed, "Dear God, thank you for my dad, mom, and big brother." I never became tired of hearing that thoughtful prayer.

Do you feel well most every day? If you do, it's something to be proud of because many don't. Some have back pains, headaches, throbbing joints, or some other pain every day. They arise with it, and it is still with them when they go to bed. Others can't sleep and are tired all the time. Still others must endure with restricted activity due to an injury. Living a long life to see and enjoy our grandchildren as they grow up is a blessing many will never have. If you have a healthy body enjoy it, but don't take it for granted.

I believe the United States is the greatest country on the face of the earth. Thousands upon thousands of people the world over dream of coming here to have an opportunity to enjoy the good life we take for granted. Most enjoy a high standard of living that makes it possible for them to have two cars in the garage, appliances to make their work easier, and money to spend for Christmas gifts. We have the privilege to go to the church of our choice, to vote for the persons we choose to represent us in government, to speak, to write, and to assemble as we please. It doesn't take a sharp person to realize we have it good in America.

Friendship should not be taken for granted either. Friends are worth more than money. We can share our true feelings with a friend. He or she is there when we need a friend most. A friend will absorb some of our hurts. Deep and meaningful friendships are a deep source of strength and pleasure and shouldn't be taken for granted either.

My house has never burned down. I have never been in a serious accident, flood, or tornado. I have never been jailed or beaten. I have never been robbed. So far I haven't had a life-threatening disease. These things may sound drastic, but they do happen to people we know. What about you? If you have been fortunate like me, don't take it for granted.

Where do we stop? This list could easily continue on to include our telephone, a pet, a pay raise, and the like. The point is: each one of us has plenty to be grateful for. Blessings should be counted.

Always Give Thanks

To remember blessings is not enough. It is good to take inventory, but we also need to stop and give thanks.

The post office maintains a "dead letter office." To it come all the letters that cannot be delivered. At Christmas, many write to Santa Claus asking for certain things. These letters are usually put in the dead letter designation.

One postal employee was interested to see how many would write to ask for things and how many would write thanking Santa for the things they received. In the three months before Christmas, there were thousands of letters asking for something. In the months after Christmas, there was only one card addressed to Santa Claus thanking him.[4]

"Thank you!" is a very small thing to say. It requires no effort to speak of, yet it brings profound joy to the ones we say it to. The simple thoughtfulness behind those two words can make another feel appreciated.

The supreme object of our gratitude, of course, is the Giver of "every good gift and every perfect gift" (Jas. 1:17). We should always give thanks unto God for his innumerable blessings.

We remember to say, "Thank you, Lord!" on Thanksgiving Day, but giving thanks is not a one-day matter. It should be an everyday affair. Saying "Thank you!" is always in season.

Thankfulness Brings Happiness

Show me a person who is ungrateful, and I'll show you a person who is miserable. I'm convinced that the thankful person is usually happy about life. A person with a grateful heart is generally happily turned.

Nancy Brandenberger observed her nine- and eleven-year-olds bickering. "You don't know how lucky you are," she said, annoyedly. "If you had to sit down and put all your blessings on paper, you couldn't find a sheet long enough!"

Listening to herself dispersing this pearl of wisdom she decided then and there to list her blessings. So each day she sat down in a quiet place and spent five minutes detailing the positive aspects of her life and closest relationships.

"My personal prayer of thanks lasted almost two weeks," she recalled. "I cannot pinpoint the day when my step became lighter and my smile more frequent. The awareness of the magnitude of my blessings was overwhelming; it put me in a positively glowing mood."[5]

I remember as a young person flying from Nashville to Orlando. The thick clouds covered the sky, making the day grey. I watched out the window as the plane ascended through the clouds. Suddenly the plane's wings broke through into the bright sunlight. There was a blanket of clouds below, but the plane glided along above them. Similarly, hardships and trials may make life look dreary, but giving thanks will help you to rise above them. It will lift your spirits above your depressing situation.

Giving thanks will contribute to our mental and emotional well-being. It will bring peace to our hearts and magnify the little that we possess.

John Henry Jowett spoke of gratitude as a vaccine and an antitoxin. As a vaccine, it prevents the invasion of a disgruntled attitude.[6] If we are thankful for the blessings of God when things are going well, it will help us build one of the best defenses against complaining and bitterness when things go badly. It can innoculate us against becoming grumpy when things don't go our way.

As an antitoxin, gratitude destroys the poison of a critical, faultfinding attitude.[7] Thankful people are less likely to badmouth others. By magnifying our own blessings we won't resent the rich blessings others possess. It will help us not to resent a friend's promotion or good fortune that it beyond our own. Instead, our gratitude will help us to marvel at God's love and goodness toward us.

Getting It All Together

A thankful person is happy. People who are genuinely grateful for their blessings are happier than those who are not. "Ingratitude" is becoming a popular personality trait. We become ungrateful when we take life and its blessings for granted, have too much pride and conceit, brood over misfortunes, and feed on envy and jealousy.

Blessings should be counted. Most of us enjoy a cozy home, nice clothes, enough to eat, a steady job, a fine family, good health, close friendships, and God's providential care, to mention a few.

But it is not enough merely to count our blessings. We should give thanks, too.

Giving thanks brings happiness. Gratitude is a vaccine that prevents a disgruntled attitude. It is an antitoxin that destroys a critical, faultfinding spirit. Giving thanks unto God for your blessings will help you to be grateful in spite of the bigger blessings of another. Gratitude cancels envy.

It would be totally unrealistic to claim that a thankful spirit would cause you to "live happily ever after" without a single disappointment, angry moment, or care in the world. Thankfulness is not a cure-all, but it will lift our spirits which makes it easier to deal with our problems. A thankful spirit is another element that brings happiness to us.

5.

Filling the Void Inside
A Spiritual Life

"I'm not going to come to church! I'm not ever going to change!" protested the man to Troy Scott, my visitation partner. We were visiting in his home, and I had been urging him and his wife to accept the Lord and to start coming to our church.

"I can identify with what you're saying," Troy broke into the conversation. "Two years ago I was just like you. But I made a change. I was always looking for something special in life, but I never could find it. Something was lacking in my life, and I didn't know what it was. Then I gave my life to Christ, and I have found it. There is a peace in my heart that only God can give. If there wasn't any heaven, if this life was all there was, I would still live for Jesus. I am so happy every day trying to live for Christ."

Have you, like Troy, always been looking for something special in life but have never completely found it? Is there something lacking in your life, and you're not exactly sure what it is? Is there an empty, restless spot in your heart that you long to fill?

You can crowd every free minute with ball games, movies, and card parties. You can ski, bowl, and golf. You can wine and dine, sightsee, vacation, and lounge around. All this and more will only bring you short-term pleasure, and soon the longing for something deeper will return.

You can't fill your inner longing with things you can buy. Suppose a rich benefactor were to say to you, "You can have anything you want that money can buy." And you start, "I want a new car, no, make it two new cars. I want to take a cruise in the Caribbean. I want a bigger house and a vacation home in the mountains. I want a closet full of the most expensive clothes. I want, I want, I want . . ." And he were to say, "It's yours, and here's enough money for you to live comfortably for the rest of your life." Would you be happy? No, not necessarily! One can get everything he wants materially and still be perfectly miserable. The problem is: peace of heart and mind doesn't necessarily come with an abundance of possessions. The things money can buy cannot fill the inner void in one's heart.

You see, within each of us there is a living soul that longs for fellowship with God, our Creator. This unrest Augustine spoke of in his famous words: *"Cor meum inquietum donec requiescat in Te, Domine."*[1] He talked about "our hearts being restless till they rest in Thee."

If you are looking for something to fill your inner longing, I have some good news and bad news for you. Hopefully, my news will not turn out like the good news-bad news story I read about. As an Air California charter flight neared Rochester on January 29, 1983, from a three-day trip to Las Vegas, a fun-loving "singing cowboy" from Waukon, Iowa, asked to speak. He thought the other passengers should recognize a woman from Harmony, Minnesota, who had won $62,000 gambling. A stewardess turned the PA system over to him. He cracked a few jokes including a good news-bad news story: "The bad news is the landing gear won't go down, and we're going to crashland. The good news is the pilot is experienced at it." But the joke went over like a lead balloon when a seventy-four-year-old woman sued Air California and the cowboy for more than $250,000 in damages, claiming she thought the plane actually was going to crash. A six member US District Court jury awarded her $10,000 in compensatory damages plus $226 in medical expenses.[2]

The Bad News

I've got good news and bad news for you. Let me tell you the bad news first. Human beings are sinners. We have made vast technological strides. We fly into outer space in a shuttle and return to land on a designated air strip. Our nation is moving toward developing a "Star Wars" military missile defense system. In the Humana Hospital in Louisville, doctors are replacing worn-out hearts with mechanical ones. Doctors can keep the human body functioning almost indefinitely with the support of machines.

We are conquering outer space but not inner space. One quick look at the headlines in almost any newspaper will convince one that human beings are sinners. More educated, prosperous, and cultured, yes, but just as much sinners. Alcoholism, divorce, and crime are increasing.

We are sinners by choice. The tendency to sin has been passed on to us from our first parents (Adam and Eve). We are sinners by our own deliberate actions. When we become old enough to make moral choices, we choose to curse, to tell a lie, or to act selfishly.

We become sinners when we fail to live up to God's standards. His standards are the Ten Commandments. In them, he tells us to worship no other gods, not to make graven images, or to take His name in vain. Remember the sabbath day, to keep it holy. Honor father and mother. Do not kill, commit adultry, steal, lie, or covet (Ex. 20:3-17). By breaking God's moral laws for right living we become sinners.

I have talked to a few folks who have rationalized they are OK. They look at other people or church members and say to themselves, *I am all right. I'm just as good as those folks*.

Watch out! The devil likes nothing better than to trick one into a false confidence. He whispers, "You are all right; you are a good person. Your moral life compares with those in the church. You don't need to change."

Satan is tricking us into getting us to measure our goodness by the wrong standard. A bad cold sounds good compared to lung cancer. When we suffer from a cold, we are sick, even though it's not cancer. The fact that we are not as bad as others does not score points with God.

Comparing ourselves to another is much like the little boy I read about who came running to his mother, shouting, "Mommy, Mommy, I'm nine feet tall!"

His mother answered, saying, "Don't talk such nonsense."

"But I really am nine feet tall," he insisted. "I measured myself."

"Well, how did you measure yourself?" she asked.

"I took off my shoe and measured myself with it. It is the same size as my foot, and I really am nine feet."

With a smile the mother replied, "Now I understand, my son, but I have to tell you that your measure was not the right one. We don't measure ourselves by the size of our feet, but we must use a 12-inch ruler."[3] Are you like the little boy? The measure for right living is not another person but the Ten Commandments.

Isaiah the prophet confessed, "All we like sheep have gone astray; we have turned every one to his own way" (Isa. 53:6). And King Solomon declared: "There is no man that sinneth not" (1 Kings 8:46). Sin harms our fellowship with God. "Your iniquities have separated between you and your God, and your sins have hid his face from you, that he will not hear" (Isa. 59:2). Without fellowship with God which He created us to have, we have an insatiable inner longing. That desire can only be filled with a restored relationship with God. You will find true happiness only when you fill the infinite abyss in your heart with God's presence. You cannot substitute a sort of do-gooderism for living according to God's laws. You say, "I'm a good sort of a fellow. I'm a decent person. Isn't that enough?"

No! No amount of good deeds on your part can even begin to cancel out your sins. You can't do enough for others to balance the scales for your wrongs. Trying to live a religious life, saying creeds, and living by certain principles won't do it either. Spiritually, you can't pull yourself up by your own bootstraps. You can no more fix your sin problem than a flat tire can fix itself. A flat tire can be fixed, but someone else must do it. You can't do it; you are helplessly separated from God because of sin. That's the bad news.

The Good News

Now, the good news! God took the initiative to restore fellowship with us by sending His own Son into the world to die for our sins. Our sins had to be atoned for, so God gave His sinless Son to die as the ultimate sacrifice for our sins.

If a rich man's son is taken by kidnappers, and they hold him until his father pays a certain price, the money is called a ransom. Sin has us in its power. God gave His Son, Jesus, to die as a ransom to free us from the slavery of sin.

Our ransom is not with "silver or gold" but with "the precious blood of Christ, as of a lamb without blemish and without spot" (1 Pet. 1:18-19). On the cross, Jesus paid the price for our deliverance.

God did this because He loves you and wanted to restore fellowship with you. His love for you is not just sentiment but action. God gave His most precious thing in the world—His only Son—for you.

The worth of a child to a father was well illustrated to me on one of my first dates. I asked a girl if she would go to the football game with me. At first, her father refused to let her go. But, after a couple of days, she told me her father wanted to see me. With fear and hesitation I went over to talk with him. After I assured him I would be very careful, he consented to let her go with me.

Then he asked, "Would you like to drive my car?" Now he was a Ford car salesman and drove a brand-new LTD. I had just turned sixteen and gotten my driver's license. Having barely become familiar with our old '55 Chevrolet, I graciously declined. Then he said something I have thought about many times since. "If I trust you with my daughter, I trust you with my car." His daughter was certainly worth far more than his new car.

God sent His only begotten Son to die for our sins to restore fellowship with us. I can't comprehend such love. But, nevertheless, He loves us that much. I can't fathom it, but the cross of Calvary is proof that He does. Forgiveness of sin is free to us, but it is not cheap. It cost God the life of His Son.

The most expensive thing God ever did was to love you and me. It cost Him a crucifixion. Creation, with its vastness and its unsearchable beauty, cost Him a word. He spoke, and the universe, with its multitude of solar systems in each galaxy, was ushered into existence. But when it came to making payment for our sins, He could not merely speak a word. It cost Him the death of His only Son. We are not redeemed by corruptible things like silver and gold. We are redeemed by the precious blood of Christ.

God took your sin bill and marked across the face of it "paid in full." If God gave His Son to atone for sins, why are people not experiencing it? God has done His part: we must do ours. It's not ours until we receive it. President Andrew Jackson pardoned George Wilson after he was sentenced to hang for mail robbery and murder. However, Wilson refused the pardon.

What to do? Chief Justice John Marshall called the Supreme Court in session to decide his fate. Marshall read the decision. "A pardon is a paper, the value of which depends upon its acceptance by the person implicated. George Wilson must be hanged." And he was. Not to accept God's forgiveness in Christ offered to you is to act as foolishly as did George Wilson.[4]

How to Make It Happen

Redemption cannot be passed down from one generation to the next. You can leave money to the next generation. You can leave a family business or a family name to others, but the forgiveness of God cannot be conveyed in this manner. To receive forgiveness of your sins and to restore fellowship with God you must:

1. *Repent of your sins*. The Bible says, "Unless you repent you will . . . perish" (Luke 13:3). To repent means to turn around. We are going in one direction, and we turn and go in the opposite direction. By nature we are going the wrong way— the way of sin—and we are to turn around and go in the opposite direction: God's way. It is a radical turning of the mind, heart, and soul from sin to God's side.

Repentance is making a 180-degree turn from sin. Let me illustrate. Suppose I were in Sebree and needed to go to Henderson, seventeen miles to the north. I drive down Main Street to Highway 41. My mind is on my busy schedule for Sunday. Not thinking, I turn right and head south instead of turning left and going north. About two miles out of town I realize I am going the wrong way. I pull in at Breeten Road and completely turn around and head in the opposite direction. We receive God's free gift of salvation by making a radical change of direction.

Repentance allows you to unclutter your hands, so you can accept God's gift. You turn loose the sin you have, so you can receive God's salvation. When you repent, you are turning from your sin so you can turn to God through faith in Jesus.

2. *Place your faith in Jesus*. The Bible teaches, "Whosoever believeth in him should not perish, but have everlasting life" (John 3:16). To believe means absolute trust. To "believe in Him" means to stake your life on Jesus for all time and eternity. Faith that results in forgiveness of sin and everlasting life is more than mental assent. It is casting yourself totally upon Him to cover your sins with His blood and to take you to heaven when you die.

The object of faith is not a body of truth called a creed, although creeds are important. Nor is the object of faith sacrifices, morals, or even yourself. The object of faith is a person: Jesus Christ. Yes, He is an historical person known as Jesus Christ, and He is the risen, living Christ!

Placing your faith in Jesus is not just believing facts about Jesus. "Thou believest that there is one God; thou doest well: the devils also believe, and tremble" (Jas. 2:19). It is not enough simply to believe historical facts about Jesus. The devils even do that. Most everyone in America believes there is a God and that Jesus is His Son. Furthermore, they would believe Jesus died for their sins and arose the third day from the grave. Is that life-changing faith? No!

The faith I am talking about has to do with commitment. It is similar to a marriage commitment. When you stand before a minister or a justice of the peace and get married, you are making a commitment to enter into a relationship with your spouse that is to last a lifetime. It is not mental assent to a contract; it is a commitment to live with a person through thick and thin, the good and the bad for a lifetime. When you place your faith in Jesus, it is a commitment to live for Him every day. Faith in Jesus is not just mere mental assent to facts about Jesus, but it is an act of entering into a personal relationship with Him as your Lord and Master for life.

You don't have to understand totally everything about the gospel in order to experience forgiveness. Ninety-nine people out of every one hundred accept the cure of an operation without being able to say how it was effected. Comparatively few of us know how electricity, a telephone, or a television work, but our lack of understanding doesn't prevent us from using and enjoying them.

To receive forgiveness and eternal life, place your total dependence on Jesus. A chair can be plenty sturdy enough to hold you up, but it never will unless you trust it enough to sit on it. The only way Jesus can deliver you from sin is for you to put your complete trust in Him.

3. *Through prayer, invite Jesus to come in and control your life*. If you are not accustomed to praying you could say a prayer similar to this. But, you must mean it with all your heart.

> Dear God,
>
> I know I have broken your Commandments and am a sinner. Please forgive me of my sins. Right now I invite Jesus to come into my life by faith. I trust Him as my Savior and will follow Him as my Lord. In Jesus' name I pray. Amen.

Come to God just as you are. Don't make excuses. Bare your soul before Him. It makes no difference what you have done. Liar, thief, drunkard, adulterer, gossip—it makes no difference. God will cleanse and forgive all who come to Him through the shed blood of Jesus. Just plead your hopelessness as a sinner, and He will cleanse each dark blot of sin in your life. Call upon Him, and He will change your life.

Don't delay! Do it today! There is an interesting story of an imaginary council of Satan and his demons. They met to devise some means of blocking people from believing upon Jesus for forgiveness of their sins. Many plans were suggested, but only one was accepted. Can you guess what it was?

It was wickedly ingenius. Here it is: to admit that the gospel of Jesus was true, to admit that God did so love us as to give His Son to die for us, to admit that we are forgiven by accepting Him as our Savior, but to suggest to all people that there is time enough later to attend to it! Put it off! Enjoy sin a while longer! Later on repent! Later on receive Jesus! Put it off![5]

Please don't let Satan trick you into waiting for a better time to repent and to believe in Jesus. Don't delay. Most people intend to get right with God, but they just put off giving their lives to Him. Don't neglect this most important matter. Do it today! Let God fill the emptiness in your life right now while you are thinking about it. You'll be eternally glad you did.

If you are empty and tired of searching for fulfillment from an inner longing, try Jesus! Only He can satisfy the hunger of your soul.

Only Jesus Christ can cancel out your imperfect human nature and restore your missing fellowship with God. A well-known story is told of a little boy who received a nice guitar for Christmas. He put his hands on the fret and held it in a fixed position while he strummed on the instrument by the hour. His father became annoyed with him and blasted, "Son, you are supposed to move your left hand up and down the fret and produce new sounds. The great guitarists do that." "Well, Dad," the boy replied, "they run their left hand up and down because they are looking for it. I found it!" When you come to Jesus and accept His gift of payment for your sins, you have found it. There is "one mediator between God and men, the man Christ Jesus" (1 Tim. 2:5).

Attend Church Regularly

After accepting Jesus Christ as your personal Savior, attend church regularly with your family. If they won't go, attend alone. You will find friends through Bible study and worship. You will discover the inspiration, instruction, and support you need to sustain life.

Recently, in a speech to the nation, President Reagan challenged Congress: "Make my day!" He was trying to push through his budget with certain cuts in programs he felt wasteful. He gave notice to the Congress: if they attached excessive programs, he would not hesitate to veto them. He quipped with pen in hand, "Make my day!"

I don't know if vetoing certain programs would make President Reagan's day or not, but I can tell you with certainty—regular church worship will "make your week!"

If you aren't accustomed to going to church each Sunday, start now. You'll like it. Worship in the church of your choice.

The Chinese proverb that was a favorite of John F. Kennedy reads, "The journey of a thousand miles begins with one step!"[6] The journey to inner satisfaction begins with one step. The first step is to accept Christ as your personal Savior. The second step is to go to church and to make it a priority in your life. Regular church attendance will help you to grow toward maturity in your faith. Don't delay. Attend the church of your choice this Sunday.

Getting It All Together

"A God-shaped vacuum" exists within you. Until it is filled, you will never be happy. You cannot find satisfaction for your inner longings in things, pleasure, or power.

Tragically, you are separated from God by your wrong deeds. The Bible calls these sin. Our sins are a wall between us and God.

Now, the good news: God took the initiative to restore fellowship with us by sending His own Son into the world to die for our sins. His shed blood on the cross is a ransom for our sins.

To fill the God-shaped vacuum you must receive Jesus Christ into your life. Here's how to make it happen.

1. *Repent of your sins*. Repentance is a strong turning of

your mind, heart, and will from all known sin. It is emptying your heart of sins, so you can replace them with Jesus. It is a radical turning of your back on sin and turning your face to Jesus.

2. *Place your faith in Jesus*. Faith in Jesus is more than just believing facts about Him. It is relying upon His sacrificial death to redeem your soul from sin. Believing in Jesus is entering into a personal, daily relationship with Him for a lifetime.

3. *Through prayer invite Jesus to come in and control your life*. He will not force His way into your life. He desires to come in, but He waits for a personal invitation. When you ask Jesus to enter your life, He comes in. Thus, you will find satisfaction for your inner longings.

After you have received Jesus Christ as your personal Savior, attend church regularly. In church you will find the inspiration, instruction, and support to sustain your faith in the Lord.

6.

Help Yourself . . .
by Helping Others
A Helping Hand

"I work hard and come home tired. They're not going to get me to help at the school carnival! Somebody else can sell the popcorn!"

"I'm not going to be an officer for the Little League. I'm not going to umpire a base at any game. I go to relax! If they can't get somebody to do everything, they should plan better. It's all I hear! Do this, do that!"

"At church it's the same. Help pass out handbills, take a survey, teach the boys' class, sing in the choir, and cook a pie for the youth fellowship."

"'I only say yes to get people off my back. I really wish they would leave me alone. My time is limited. I'm tired, and I don't appreciate other people bugging me! Why can't I be left alone?"

Do you ever feel like that?

You may feel like saying, "If only I could go to community and church activities and be left alone, I would be a lot happier. I would enjoy things more if I didn't have to get involved."

Wrong! Instead of finding happiness and fulfillment you will only be cutting yourself off from others. You may look out just for "number one," but that's not the way to happiness.

Former First Lady Rosalynn Carter regularly visited centers for the mentally ill and the elderly. On these trips she found men and women, old and young, volunteering their services. She was commending a group of elderly volunteers for helping in a Massachusetts public school when someone said to her, "When you're all wrapped up in yourself, you're a very small package."[1] A self-centered person is a very small package, indeed!

Happiness is illusive to those who seek it. The more you pursue it, the harder it is to find. So stop chasing and start giving yourself to others through service, and happiness will come to you. Michelle Randolph observed, "Happiness is like a butterfly. The more you chase it, the more it eludes you. But if you turn your attention to other things, it will come and softly sit on your shoulder."[2]

Willingly give yourself in service to help others, and you will be happier than you ever imagined. Don't worry about doing more than your share or about who gets the credit. Help out even if you are tired. Giving a helping hand is another avenue to happiness!

Others, Community Organizations, and the Church Need Your Help

Other people need your help. Look around! The sick in your community need someone to do laundry, cook meals, and pick up prescriptions for them. Shut-ins need someone to bring the groceries and visit them. The elderly need someone to read to them, quilt with them, and help clean for them. The handicapped need someone to mop the floor and to take them shopping. Those isolated with a retarded child need a friend with whom to share their burden. People are hungry for someone to listen to their concerns and to share their hurts. Will you be that someone?

Catastrophes are no respecter of persons. You may think,

I've got the world by the tail! Then a fire, a storm, or a wreck can literally wipe you out. When the unexpected strikes, people in your community need all the help they can get. You can prepare food for workers, help clean your city streets, pitch in, and assist a family setting up housekeeping again. You can be there to listen and comfort. "A friend in need is a friend, indeed!"

When others need help, do you pitch in and help or do nothing? When help is needed, do you rationalize, *I'm too tied-up and tired, and, besides, other folks have more free time than I do*"? Do you stand on the sideline, saying to yourself, *Nobody helped me when my house flooded. Why should I help them?*

Many community organizations need your help, too. Without volunteer help, these organizations could not function.

Hospitals and nursing homes continuously need volunteer workers. Hospital volunteers answer the phone and give information, assist families in the surgery waiting room, do clerical work in admittance, push patients to their cars as they are discharged, deliver flowers and mail, sell magazines and snacks, and do much more. Without volunteers who willingly give of their time and energy, many of these extra services would have to be cut drastically.

Volunteers also make life appreciably better for nursing home residents. They assist with craft projects, birthdays, and holiday parties. Volunteers, young and old, read to those with poor eyesight. Others run errands for the immobile. Many community folks use their talents to entertain and provide church services for the residents. Many others give their time to visit the lonely and discouraged. Volunteers provide invaluable services without which many residents would never know someone cares about them.

Your church also needs your help: singers for the choir; teachers for Bible and Christian education classes; committee members to plan and coordinate activities, prepare the budget, and nominate the volunteer workers; individuals as greeters, ushers, and hostesses; some to keep the building and grounds attractive and in good repair; and everyone to contact absentees and enlist the unchurched. The list of ways and areas where your help is needed is extensive. Almost any talent and interest you have can be used of God through the church.

God is depending on us to do His work. He could have used steam power, atomic power, or angelic power to do His work on earth, but He didn't. He uses people. God has always harnessed human power to do His work, and He still does.

> Christ has no hands but our hands
>   To do His work today;
> He has no feet but our feet
>   To lead men in His way;
> He has no tongues but our tongues
>   To tell men how He died;
> He has no help but our help
>   to lead them to His side.[3]

It has been said, "Without God we cannot, and without us God will not." God has chosen to do His work on earth through people. I am reminded of the story of the preacher who stood admiring the green fields of corn and beans, the clean fence rows and well-maintained buildings. He commented to the farmer, "The Lord sure has given you a beautiful farm!" "Yes, but you should have seen it when the Lord had it all by Himself!" replied the farmer.

Did you know that God has problems recruiting enough human power to do His work? A second-grade teacher asked, "Johnny, what is your favorite parable?" He enthusiastically replied, "The one where somebody loafs and fishes."

That sounds like some people, doesn't it? They loaf when there is work to be done. And when someone else does it, they fish for the compliments, giving the impression that "we" have done a good job.

Folks all around you need help. Offer your services today. Volunteer; get involved. Don't wait to be begged.

It is amazing what we can do when we really want to. It is equally amazing how many excuses we can find for not doing this or that. We can play ball with a fever, go hunting with aches and pains, and party after a hard day's work. But if we don't want to do something, we suddenly realize: "My feet hurt; it's raining; I'm too busy; I'm too inexperienced; I'm too old or too young. Get somebody else. A whole lot of folks can do that better than me." The list of excuses can be endless.

I heard of a man who asked his neighbor, "May I borrow your rope?"

The neighbor gave a weird reply: "No, I'm using it to tie up milk!"

"But, you can't tie milk with a rope!"

"I know," the neighbor quipped, "but when you don't want to do something, one reason's about as good as another."

What about you? Can you be counted on to serve willingly, or do you do as little as possible? If you are doing a bare minimum, you are losing the joy and satisfaction of serving. I challenge you: resolve to help out anyway you can. Don't restrain yourself. Pour out your energy in service. Freely help. Don't worry about being taken advantage of. Helping others is a superlative use of your time and energy.

Fringe Benefits of Helping

Helping others often goes unnoticed. Getting involved in community organizations and church work takes time and energy. Even though your help and service may seem unappreciated, don't hesitate to lend a hand. The fringe benefits are considerable. Let's count them.

More Meaning in Life

First, by helping out you gain more meaning in life. Many people don't have anything meaningful to do. I am reminded of the old couple whose life had been characterized by poverty. They went to a county fair. The merry-go-round caught the attention of the man. He wanted to ride it and discussed the venture with his wife. She discouraged and poked fun at him. But he bought the ticket, mounted his horse, and rode until the music ran down.

As he walked off, his wife was waiting for him with her arms crossed. "Now look at you!" she thundered. "You spent your money! You rode the thing! You got off where you got on, and you ain't been nowhere yet!"

Are the things you are doing no more meaningful than that? Do you get off where you got on and accomplish nothing in the journey?

Sometimes it is hard to sift out what is vital in life. An old riddle says, "As I was going to Saint Ives, I met a man with seven wives. Each wife had seven sacks. Each sack had seven cats. Each cat had seven kits. Kits, cats, sacks, and wives: How many were going to Saint Ives?" In spite of all the kits, cats, sacks, and wives along the road, only one man was headed to Saint Ives. We must be careful not to spend our time in meaningless activities and cluttered agendas.

Helping others gives us an added sense of meaning in life. One of the best investments we can make is to give freely our time and energy in helping children, the elderly, the sick—anyone with problems. Helping others pays in dividends of a more meaningful life.

Let me tell you a secret! The church members who become involved and participate are the happiest Christians. The meaningful Christian life is found through serving.

Back when George W. Truett pastored First Baptist Church,

Dallas, he preached a message on "The Secret of Happiness." He proclaimed that the way to happiness was through accepting Christ as Savior and serving Him as Lord. A young millionaire bachelor known for his flamboyant life-style responded.

Some six months later, the young man came to Truett and moaned, "Dr. Truett, you misled me. You led me to believe if I would accept Christ I would be happy. I am anything but happy. I used to enjoy drinking, gambling, and carousing, but I don't now. I have too much respect for the church to do these things while I still belong. So I want my name taken off the church rolls, so I can return to the kind of life I used to enjoy."

"Young man," Truett replied, "I don't have the right to take your name off the church rolls, but I think I know your trouble. If you will do one thing I ask you to do, and you still want your name off the church rolls, I'll ask the church in conference to remove it." When the young millionaire agreed, the pastor shared that he had just learned of a poor widow whose family was in desperate need. He asked that the man buy a basket of groceries and take them to the family and then return to the pastor's study to talk with him.

Loaded with groceries the millionaire went to the shanty. As he approached the door he heard someone crying. He listened. The widow was weeping and praying, "O, God, send us bread. Send us something to eat. We are dying from hunger."

He wanted to set the groceries at the door and leave, but fearing she might not find the food for sometime, he knocked. Upon opening the door, she was overcome with joy. She cried, "Mister, you are an angel from heaven!" The little children put their arms around his knees and loved him as they began to eat the goodies. He was embarrassed at their emotions and said, "I must go."

"No, you can't go until we have bowed and thanked God for this food," the widow insisted.

She and the children fell to their knees. The millionaire

knelt, too. Thinking him to be a spiritual man, she asked him to pray first. He had never prayed in the presence of others but made a stab at it. He thanked God for the privilege of helping someone in need. Then the widow and children thanked God for the food and the good man.

The bachelor hurried back to Truett's study and said, "Pastor, I don't want my name off the church roll. I know my trouble now. I just want something more to do for God."[4]

Helping others gives meaning to one's life. It makes one feel useful.

Personal Joy Increases

Second, by helping out, your personal joy increases. It makes you feel good to help other people. A man tells of a childhood experience he cherishes. "I was in the living room listening to the radio, when my dad came in from shoveling snow. He looked thoughtfully at me and said, 'In twenty-four hours, you won't even remember what you are listening to now. How about doing something for the next twenty minutes that you will remember for the next twenty years? I promise that you will enjoy it every time you think of it.'"

"What is it?" I asked.

"Well, son, there are several inches of snow on old Mrs. Brown's walk. Why don't you see if you can shovel it off and get back home without her knowing."

"I went over and did the walk in about fifteen minutes. She never knew who did it. Dad was right. It has been a lot more than twenty years, and I have enjoyed the memory every time I have thought about it."[5]

Getting involved in community activities also adds to your enjoyment. Years ago my friend, Hugh Tow, coached a group of Little League boys in Sebree. He told of a statement his friend Ed Hust made while coaching some boys from Providence. It went about like this: "Coaching Little League boys is the next best thing to playing yourself. You experience all the thrills of it again through the boys."

Your enjoyment in church increases as you get involved. One afternoon Harold Dye, well-known author of *The Prophet of Little Cane Creek,* sat on the porch with Brother A. S. Petry, pioneer preacher in the Cumberland Mountains. He asked Petry, "What is the greatest thing that has happened to you during your long ministry in the mountains?"

Pointing to the church nearby Petry said, "Two Sundays ago I was guest of honor at services held at the church. As we entered, the ushers gave each person a red rose. I was given a seat on the platform.

"When the services were almost over, the pastor asked me to stand. He then said to the congregation, 'If Brother Petry was the one responsible for your finding Christ as your Savior, come up and pin your rose on him.'

"They started coming from every part of the room. They pinned roses all over my coat, down my pants legs, all over my back. I felt like a blooming idiot. But I would not trade those roses for all the coal beneath the surface of the land and all the gold in Fort Knox."[6]

So get involved. Don't just be a spectator! Get out of the stands and into the ball game. When you put on the pads and uniform and get into the game, you may get bumped around a little, but that is far more fun than sitting in the stands and not being a part of the action.

Don't hesitate to give a helping hand. You'll be glad you did. Simply knowing you helped to make something good happen for somebody else can bring you great joy.

Personally Profit

Third, by helping out others you will personally profit in the long run. Dr. Norman Vincent Peale told this story. While in

Florida some years ago, he met a man who appeared quite ill. He had been driven down from the North by his own private chauffeur. He had three nurses with him for round-the-clock care. The man's doctor told Peale, "Nothing's wrong with him. I do not have any medicine that will help him. He is so self-centered and so worried about himself, he just makes himself sick. I wish you could help him, Dr. Peale."

One day, while sitting with the man on the porch at the resort, Peale saw an older woman trying to carry a chair up the steps. She had gotten the runners hooked under the bannister and couldn't get the chair loose.

Peale suggested to the man, "Go over and help that woman."

"I can't. I'm sick."

"Go on, you can do it."

The man argued, "You do it. You are younger than I am."

Finally, the man hobbled over and grunted and groaned as he helped the woman. Then he held the chair while she sat down in it. She profusely thanked him.

After the man came back and sat down, Peale asked, "How do you feel?"

"Well, I don't feel as bad as I thought I did."

"See there, I told you you'd feel better when you help someone else," Peale encouraged.

"Oh, that's silly!" the man remarked.

"Well," Peale continued, "the Bible says, 'Whosoever will save his life shall lose it: and whosoever will lose his life for my sake shall find it'! That is what you have just done."

The man said, "I have heard that all my life, but I never knew what it meant. I do feel better. I got a kick out of that. I believe that is true. I understand."

The story has a happy ending. Peale concluded, "I was back there a couple of years later and saw a man in the hall, striding along, shoulders back, head up. He grabbed my arm and said, 'Hello, Dr. Peale!' I looked at him and said, 'It can't be! It's you! Where are your nurses?' 'I don't need my nurses,' he replied, I am all well. I am as sound as a dollar and feeling great. I have been doing what Jesus said to do.'"[7]

You can't help others without helping yourself. As you pour yourself out in service to others you will find yourself extremely happy. A bulletin insert gave ten rules for getting rid of the blues: "Go out and do something for someone else and repeat it nine times."[8] That just about hits the nail on the head, doesn't it?

If we go out of our way to help others, usually they will remember our kindness and will try to return it. This is illustrated by Roone Arledge, long-time head of ABC's news and sports divisions, as he explains how he got his first break in television.

"During college summer vacations I worked at an inn in Chatham, Massachusetts. One night a family had driven a long way, and when they arrived, the dining room was closed. The hostess refused to seat them, but, as headwaiter, I interposed. 'I can't let you be disappointed. Come in, and I'll wait on you.' They were very grateful and before they left they took my name. The day I walked into the office at DuMont television (a pioneering network), the man in charge of programming looked up and asked, 'How's everything at the Wayside Inn?' It turned out that he was the person who had driven down for dinner that summer night, and he had never forgotten that I stayed to wait on him. From the instant he recognized me, I knew I had the job."[9]

The universal law of cause and effect is activated when you help others. The basketball player yelled to the ball hog on the team, "Don't be afraid to pass it; that way you will get a pass in return." When you help others, they might well help you. The good you do for others is remembered and is often reciprocated. Oftentimes, it comes back to you with compounded interest.

Eternal Rewards

Fourth, by helping others you will receive eternal rewards. If no one ever reciprocates for your good deeds or hours of service, don't worry. If you don't ever receive a thank you for your labors of love, don't let it upset you. After all, you shouldn't be helping others for recognition or for anything in return. You should help others and work in community projects, organizations, and church purely because you care and want to help out.

Just remember this: no matter how obscure your help may seem, God sees and knows, and one day He will reward you for it. When you are helping others who are in need, you are serving the Lord just as directly as if you were doing church work. Jesus declared, "For I was hungry and you fed me; I was thirsty and you gave me water; I was a stranger and you invited me into your homes; naked and you clothed me; sick and in prison, and you visited me." The righteous asked when did they do those things for Him. He lauded, "When you did it to these my brothers you were doing it to me!" (Matt. 25:36-40, TLB). Furthermore, He exclaimed, "And if, as my representatives, you give even a cup of cold water to a little child, you will surely be rewarded" (Matt. 10:42, TLB).

One day the Lord will say to those who have served Him, "Well done, thou good and faithful servant: . . . enter thou into the joy of thy Lord" (Matt. 25:21). Work for the Lord may not pay much, but, just remember, the retirement plan is out of this world! God's rewards to those who serve Him are beyond imagination. "Eye hath not seen, nor ear heard, neither have entered into the heart of man, the things which God hath prepared for them that love him" (1 Cor. 2:9).

Life is so uncertain. Some things we can do almost anytime, but some others will never be done unless we grasp the chance when it comes. For these it is either *now* or *never!* When you are moved to do a good deed, help someone in trouble, or to serve the Lord, do it. Seize the moment. We will not pass this way again. Helping others and working in community organizations and in your church produces the fringe benefits of personal meaning, joy, and eternal rewards.

Getting It All Together

Looking out for "number one" may be the way to the top, but it isn't the way to happiness. Thinking only about yourself, continually expecting to be appreciated, and doing as little as possible for others is the way to be perfectly miserable. When you're all wrapped up in yourself, you're a very small package.

To be happy learn to serve. Willingly help anyone who needs it. Do anything that needs to be done. Don't hold back. Look around! Other folks, community organizations, and the church need your help. Lend a hand.

The fringe benefits of helping out are large. Let's count them.

1. *We gain more meaning in life.* A lot of things we do don't amount to much. But helping others is beneficial, and it gives us a sense of purpose and usefulness.

2. *Our personal joy increases.* There is more enjoyment in getting involved in a project than just watching. We get the enjoyment of accomplishment and excitement of making it happen.

3. *We personally profit in the long run.* When we go out of our way to help others, usually they will remember our kindness and will try to return it. Helping others will eventually help us. "Cast thy bread upon the waters," and "after many days" it will return (Eccl. 11:1).

4. *We will receive eternal rewards.* Other folks might forget our helpful deeds, but they do not go unnoticed. God sees and remembers and rewards in due time. One day He will reward us eternally for our kindness to others and for our hard work through His church.

Lend a helping hand to others, to your community organizations, and to the church, and you will be happier than you ever imagined. Don't worry about doing more than your share. The fringe benefits of serving are outstanding. Lend a helping hand; it's an avenue to happiness.

7.

Latch Onto the Affirmative
A Positive Outlook

"Easy Street"! As I drove south on Highway 41 from Henderson to Sebree, I saw it. The street into Robards Heights is named "Easy Street." One block east "Heavenly Place" connects into "Easy Street." Have you ever dreamed of someday living at the corner of "Easy Street" and "Heavenly Place"? I have!

The government warning against mail fraud states: "If it sounds too good to be true, it probably is." It sounds good, figuratively speaking, to live at the corner of "Easy Street" and "Heavenly Place," and, sure enough, it is too good to be true.

As a matter of fact, you will never live at the corner of "Easy Street" and "Heavenly Place"—not in this life anyway. Life is anything but rosy. Bad things happen to all of us.

You may think, *If I love God and serve Him, nothing bad will happen to me.* You may feel that if you tithe, pray, and do your best everyday, then you will enjoy a safe, easy life. Let me tell you frankly, "It just isn't so!"

An outstanding Christian woman called to inform us that her husband had just died. He was forty-seven and had been in the hospital for two weeks. Now, she is left a widow.

Bad things happen to good people as well as to anyone else.

Marie was stunned as Charles returned from a business trip to tell her, "I have spent the entire week deciding how to tell you that our marriage is over." Their marriage was terminated after twenty-six years.

The doctor's words sounded unreal to Les, "Your wife and little girl died at the initial impact of the vehicles." The hurt was so deep!

Bad things happen to all of us. If you have seemingly been spared, brace yourself. One of these days, it will come to you, too. Often bad things happen at the most unexpected moments, and, quite often, sooner than we expect. So, just prepare to face bad times sooner or later. They come to everyone. And you and I are not immune.

The clue to living a happy life is not the difference between having good things happen to you and having bad things happen to you. It has to do with how you deal with what happens to you. You can let your hardships make you bitter and cynical, or you can grow wiser and stronger from them. You can either let the bad things destroy you, or you can use them to develop noble qualities in your life. It's up to you.

You can salvage good out of bad times. Here's how.

Lean on God

When hard times are pressing in on you, lean on God. He will help you. The adult choir in our church sings, "How Big Is God?" by Stuart Hamblen. The chorus goes: "How big is God? . . . He's big enough to rule the mighty universe, yet, small enough to live within my heart."

How big is God? He's big enough to help you. One day a little boy stepped out against a mighty giant. The giant had tremendous armor. He stood nine feet, six-inches tall. His armor weighed 157 pounds. The head of his spear weighed nineteen pounds, and the shaft was the size of a weaver's beam. The young boy took a slingshot and five small, smooth stones. What was that against so much? Not a fair battle, just a small boy against an experienced giant warrior? Not really! When God took over the sling and directed the stone, then it was not a fair battle for the giant!

How big is God? He's big enough to meet your need. Paul affirmed, "My God shall supply all your need according to his riches in glory by Christ Jesus" (Phil. 4:19). An old, black man mused, "There's no need to worry. Everytime the Lord makes another possum, he just plants another persimmon tree." He's big enough to supply your need.

Violet's father died the summer after her freshman year in college. So she stayed home to work on the farm that summer rather than in town to earn money for the next year's schooling. Her mother and younger brothers and sisters became Christians that summer. As Violet began to worry about the next year's tuition, her mother kept saying something would come up, and a way would be provided.

About two weeks before time for the fall semester to begin, one of her high school teachers came out to the farm to tell Violet that she had submitted her name to the city's Chamber of Commerce as a possible recipient for a $500 school grant. Of the ten names submitted, Violet's was chosen.

Ladies in the community from their church had made seven new outfits for her to start back to school. They surprised her with them that same week.

Before Christmas, the ladies in her community from the Baptist Church and the Methodist Church got together and had a silver tea in her honor. They sent her a check for $112 along with a beautiful, white silk handmade book in which each of the ladies present had signed and written her a personal word of encouragement.

I don't understand how it happens, but it does. This world

was created and is sustained by a generous God. He wants the best for all His children. He made it so that His bountiful supply will come to help us meet our needs.

I am not suggesting you can be lazy or idle or fail to provide for the future and expect God to take care of you. God takes care of the birds and the squirrels, but He doesn't put the seeds and nuts into their mouths. The birds have to search to find the seeds, and the squirrels have to store nuts for winter. If you want to eat, you must work.

"How big is God? . . . He's big enough to rule the mighty universe, yet small enough to live within my heart." Jesus assured His disciples, "Are not two sparrows sold for a farthing? and one of them shall not fall on the ground without your Father. But the very hairs of your head are all numbered. Fear ye not therefore, ye are of more value than many sparrows" (Matt. 10:29-31).

Who would be interested in how many hairs are on your head? The exact number is not important. The point Jesus was making is: nothing about your life is too minute or unimportant for God to care about. God loves you and is ready to help you.

His power is available to anyone who calls upon Him. Jesus explained, "Ask, and it shall be given you; seek, and ye shall find; knock, and it shall be opened unto you: For every one that asketh receiveth; and he that seeketh findeth; and to him that knocketh it shall be opened. . . . If ye then, being evil, know how to give good gifts unto your children, how much more shall your Father which is in heaven give good things to them that ask him?" (Matt. 7:7-8,11).

There was a woman who was well known in her own area for her simple faith and her great calmness in the midst of trials. Another woman living at a distance, hearing of her, said, "I must go and see that woman and learn the secret of her strong and happy life."

The seeker inquired, "Are you the woman with the great

faith?" "No," she replied, "I am not the woman with the great faith, but I am the woman with the little faith in the great God."

Our extremity is God's opportunity. During the Exodus from Egypt, the Israelites were trapped between the sea and the pursuing Egyptian army. Just when they appeared to be hopelessly caught, God made a way for the Israelites through the sea. He opened up the sea and overthrew the forces of Pharaoh (Ex. 14:16-27). God is able to overrule events and adverse circumstances for His people. When your situation appears hopeless, God can and will open a way if you will trust Him.

When bad things happen to you, lean on God. He can open up a way. Moses called for the people to stand firm and see what God would do. He made a way across the sea when there was none. God is still in the business of opening a way when we see none.

This does not mean God is going to make things easy or rosy for you. Jesus invites us to lean on Him, but He doesn't offer to take our load from us. "Come unto me," Jesus said, "all ye that labour and are heavy laden, and I will give you rest. Take my yoke upon you, and learn of me; for I am meek and lowly in heart: and ye shall find rest unto your souls. For my yoke is easy, and my burden is light" (Matt. 11:28-30). He offers to help you in the midst of your hard times. A yoke is for two. He will pull alongside you.

The load may seem unbearable, but you can be assured the Lord will never ask you to pull more than you are able. When you are weary, lean on God.

Adopt a Positive Attitude

Next, adopt a positive attitude. Granted, everything isn't going to be rosy. The saintliest people get cancer, ulcers, and arthritis. Hard times are no respecter of persons. But, in spite of these—refuse to be negative.

Some people go through life having the habit of looking at the

negative side of everything instead of at the positive. A lady
came up to Evangelist E. J. Daniels after one of his revival cru-
sades. She said, "I understand that you are a marriage counselor. I want you to talk to my husband. I'm dissatisfied with
that man!"

Detecting that she needed counseling too, Daniels told her,
"I won't talk to him unless he wants me to, and unless you are
in on the conference." She replied, "I'll have him here tomorrow night!"

Sure enough, the next night she was sitting in the audience
with her husband. He looked like a midget beside her. She
looked to be 300 pounds, and he might have weighed 90 pounds
sopping wet!

After the service, she grabbed him by the hand and dragged
him down the aisle like a lamb to the slaughter. Suspecting the
conference might become embarrassing, Daniels suggested
they sit in his car. At the car, she opened the door and put him
in the back seat, and she got in on the front seat with Daniels.

Turning around and facing her husband, the woman began
shaking her finger in his face. She complained about a dozen
things about him. All of them were insignificant criticisms.

Finally, tired of her tirade, Daniels interrupted, "Lady, the
criticisms you are aiming against your husband don't amount to
a 'hill of beans' compared to the complaints that most wives
have against their husbands. Let me ask you some questions:
Does your husband ever try to beat you up?" "No, Brother
Daniels, he has never laid a hand on me to hurt me."

Then he asked, "Is your husband kind to the children?"
"Brother Daniels, he is the kindest father you ever saw. He is so
nice to the children."

He continued, "Does your husband support you?"

Her answer was, "This is one of the good things about him.
He always comes home and gives me the paycheck."

After several similar questions, Daniels summarized,

"Lady, you have one of the nicest husbands that I have ever heard about."

She smiled and said, "You know, Brother Daniels, he ain't so bad after all!"[1]

Her problem was: she was looking at what she thought were the faults of her husband, and she totally overlooked his many good points. She was emphasizing the negatives and ignoring the positives! If we are not careful, we will get into the same habit.

Negative persons don't see the sky. They focus on the clouds. They concentrate on the specks of dust and fail to see the masterpiece. They look for failure instead of success.

If you expect to find bad things, you probably will. What we anticipate and look for we usually find.

The investor who focuses on the negative outlook of the stock market sees bad omens on the horizon and reacts with too much caution. Without realizing it, he makes failure more likely than success.

Adopt a positive attitude. Believe the best is about to come your way and that something exciting is right around the corner. Your planning and expectancy will help it to come true. What we look for and work for usually happens.

Greet each day with optimism. Be a "Good morning, Lord" kind of person instead of a "Good Lord, morning" person. Each morning declare, "This is the day which the Lord hath made; we will rejoice and be glad in it" (Ps. 118:24). Granted, in it you may experience difficulties, pain, and trials, but don't let them defeat you. Approach the day with confidence that you can handle whatever it brings.

"He who believes he can—can and will."[2] Make this a basic approach toward life. Come to believe as the apostle Paul said, "I can do all things through Christ which strengtheneth me" (Phil. 4:13). One plus God equals enough!

One plus God is equal to any task. The song "High Hopes"

has a line, "Everybody knows an ant can't move a rubber tree plant." But the ant believes he can, and the next line notes, "Oops, there goes another rubber tree plant!"

Adopt a positive attitude toward life. God is in charge, and life can be good. The good things in life far outweigh the bad. There are far more sunrises than cyclones.[3]

Turn the Hard Knocks into Blessings

Then, work at turning the hard knocks of life into blessings. Hard knocks can't be avoided. They are a part of life. An unexpected job layoff couldn't have come at a worse time with Christmas only two months away. A company transfer sent your family into a tailspin. A back injury makes it impossible for you to do your job. The baby you had long anticipated is born with Downs Syndrome. You don't choose whether or not you will have troubles. You can only choose how they will affect you.

If you don't allow yourself to become bitter and filled with self-pity, your trials and hardships can temper your character, as metal in a furnace, to make you into a better person. Three-year-old Louie Braille was in his father's shop when a tool slipped and went into his eye. Because of poor hygiene, infection got into it. As little Louie rubbed his eyes, he transferred the infection into the other eye. He ended up totally blind. Braille could have become embittered over his experiences and helped no one. But as the years passed, he learned from his blindness to help other blind persons to read. At age fifteen he invented a system of writing by punching holes in paper and fashioned a new method of reading by touch. This system bears his name.[4]

Fanny Crosby, the great hymn writer, was blinded because a well-meaning, but ignorant, doctor tried to treat an infection with hot poultices on her eyes. She could have become bitter and hated the doctor and blamed God for letting it happen. Instead, she poured out a fountain of joy and praise all her life long. Her hardship tempered her character, and she has blessed succeeding generations with her triumphant hymns: "To God Be the Glory," "Redeemed, How I Love to Proclaim It!," "All the Way My Savior Leads Me," and hundreds of others.[5] Bad times color life, but you can choose the color.

What will you do with your hard knocks? Will you let them defeat you, or will you turn them into a blessing? An oyster goes through life, dies, and accomplishes nothing—unless it gets hurt. If some gravel or grit get inside the shell wounding it, the oyster begins to coat the internal wound, producing a gorgeous valuable pearl.

We grow the most not from the smooth, easy-sailing times but from the storms of life. Usually it doesn't occur to us that God is able to take our troubles and actually do something good in our lives with them. Many of the most ennobling qualities of those we most admire were developed in the difficult times of their lives.

George W. Truett, predecessor to W. A. Criswell at First Baptist Church, Dallas, was out quail hunting with his best friend, the police chief of that city. Truett accidentally shot and killed his best friend. Even though Truett has been deceased for years, many can still remember the pathos in his voice as clearly as if it were today. Perhaps his compassion for his congregation stemmed from the tragedy of that accident.[6]

In the hard times you learn best how to live. The poet expressed it well:

> I walked a mile with Pleasure;
>   She chattered all the way,
> But left me none the wiser
>   For all she had to say.

I walked a mile with Sorrow
   And ne'er a word said she;
But oh, the things I learned from her
When Sorrow walked with me!
    —Robert Browning Hamilton

I am not saying everything that happens to us is good. Nor is everything that happens to us God's will. Kenneth Chafin walked into a hospital room where a young woman had suffered a miscarriage. He had known her and her husband for quite some time. They had planned, talked, and dreamed about what this child would mean to them and would be in the world. Chafin took her by her hand and said, "I am sorry, Carolyn."

She replied, "This is what God wanted."

"Carolyn," Chafin responded, "I cannot believe that. Just because you are a minister's wife, you think you are supposed to bow down and say everything that happens is what God wants. I do not think God got up this morning and said, 'I am going to take Carolyn's baby.' Not everything that happens is good. And not everything that happens is of God."[7]

Certainly, not everything that happens is good or of God. But you can learn something good from it if you turn to God in it. God can help you in the midst of your pain, your anger, your questions, to begin salvaging something good out of the calamity that has happened to you.

Maybe you're thinking, *I don't believe that*. But wait, it's true. The Scripture promises, "We know that all things work together for good to them that love God, to them who are the called according to his purpose" (Rom. 8:28).

A disappointment, a frustration, or a setback may be a time of profound personal growth. Don't waste a trouble. Ask God to help you learn from your bad experiences, so you can help someone else.

Remember, not everything that happens to you is God's will, and much that happens is not good, but some good can come out of it. Look for the good that can come from the bad and learn from it, so you can become a better, stronger person.

After receiving forty years of training as an Egyptian prince, Moses killed an Egyptian and fled for his life to the desert of Midian. There he settled down to family life and to shepherding the flocks of his father-in-law. To all appearances, his sudden act of passion in Egypt had permanently closed the door of his service to God there.

During the long years that followed, it seemed as though all Moses' excellent training had been for nothing. But unknown to Moses, he was learning to cope with the rigorous life in the very desertland through which he would later lead the Israelites. During all this time in Midian the future leader of Israel had time to meditate, to learn patience, and to develop strength of character and will.

God works out His will for our lives in mysterious ways. What we call a detour may be the most important part of the trip. God is a God of economy. He doesn't waste anything.

A disaster in our lives can be turned into a blessing. It can force us out of old patterns and cause us to move on to a higher level of life. The Enterprise, Alabama, town square has a monument to the boll weevil. In 1915 the boll weevil devastated Coffee County. The economy of this rich land that produced cotton had made wealthy farmers out of everybody; therefore, the boll weevil just wiped them out. It was a disaster. That was when they said, "We must diversify." Now they grow peanuts, soybeans, and other crops, and prosperity has returned to the land. So the citizens of Coffee County erected a monument to the boll weevil. It shook them loose from sole dependence upon cotton to diversified farming and on to new prosperity.[8]

Turn the hard knocks into blessings. Don't let the tough times defeat you or make you bitter. You can't control many things that happen to you, but you can control how you will react to them. "If life gives you a lemon, make lemonade." Use the hard knocks as stepping stones to strengthen your character and to live a more productive life.

Live Just One Day at a Time

Also, learn to live just one day at a time. Christy Lane made popular the song "One Day at a Time." She puts deep feeling into its lyrics because of her many disappointments. Her testimony is that over the years she had learned to live just "One Day at a Time."[9] Those touching lyrics remind us we can't live more than one day at once.

"Yesterday's gone!" It's mistakes, cares, blunders, heartaches, and pains are passed forever beyond our recall. No amount of money can bring back yesterday. We can't undo a single act. Nor can we erase a single word. Yesterday's gone. So stop trying to relive it. Get on with living today. Close the door on the past. "And tomorrow may never be mine," the lyrics continue. So don't worry about the future. It's senseless. Most of the things we worry about never happen. And those that do are seldom as bad as we imagine.

I heard the story of a grandfather clock that had been sitting in the hallway for two generations, keeping time—tick tock, tick tock. One day the clock had a nervous breakdown. The clock went to the clock psychiatrist, and he came in just shattered.

The clock psychiatrist inquired, "What is the matter with you?"

"I have just broken down—I've got too much on me—I can't stand it any longer—I just can't face it."

"Well, what is it? What do you do?"

"I sit in that hall, and I go tick tock, tick tock."

"That doesn't seem to be a problem"

"You just don't understand! I have to make two ticks a second: that is 120 ticks a minute—7,200 ticks an hour! That is 172,800 ticks a day! Why, that's 1,209,600 ticks in one single week: more than 62 million ticks a year! And I can't tick 62 million ticks. I'm all worn out!"

The clock psychiatrist asked, "How many ticks do you have to tick at a time?"

"I just have to tick one."

"Why don't you try ticking one tick at a time?"

And so the old clock went back and tried it—just ticking one tick at a time, and that was twenty years ago. He is still ticking along without any problems, one tick at a time!

That is a silly story. Yet some people try to live ten days at a time—thirty days at a time—365 days at a time.

Centuries ago, Jesus gave a simple prescription that costs nothing at the pharmacy. Here it is, "Take therefore no thought for the morrow: . . . Sufficient unto the day is the evil thereof" (Matt. 6:34). Worrying about tomorrow will place a cloud over today's sunshine. It will cause you to overlook all the wonderful things God is doing for you today. Tomorrow will take care of itself when it comes. So take Jesus' advice, and don't worry about the future.

Stop worrying. It has never solved a problem, paid a debt, or lightened a burden. It is counterproductive. So quit worrying and start living!

Live today just as excitedly as you would a vacation day. Don't wait until a holiday, a weekend, a vacation, or even retirement to enjoy life. Celebrate today as a very special day. Enjoy Monday, Tuesday, Wednesday, etc., as much as if it were the weekend. Don't wait until tomorrow to enjoy life. Live every day to its fullest. Seize every minute. Really live it. Don't be afraid to do something different or to try something new. You may not get to live the tomorrow you were planning for.

Getting It All Together

Hard times come to all of us. Bad things happen to everyone. Accidents, illness, unemployment, and grief are no respecter of persons. They come to good people as well as bad. Living a happy life is not the difference between having good things happen to you as opposed to bad things happening to you. It has to do with how you deal with what happens to you. You can let your hardships make you bitter and cynical, or you can use them to help you become a stronger and better person. Here's how:

1. *Lean on God*. He will help you. "He's big enough to rule the mighty universe, yet small enough to live within my heart." His power is available to you, and He wants to help you. So call on Him.

2. *Adopt a positive attitude*. Refuse to be negative. Believe the best is about to come your way. Greet each day as a new opportunity. "You plus God" are equal to any task.

3. *Turn the hard knocks into blessings*. Don't let hardships cause self-pity. Turn your sorrow, suffering, and problems into stepping stones. Remember the oyster. You, too, can turn an irritation into something beautiful in your life. Overcoming hardships can be God's means of helping you strengthen your character.

4. *Live just one day at a time*. You can't change a mistake, blunder, heartache, or erase a single word of the past. Yesterday's gone. So stop trying to relive it. Don't worry about what will happen in the future, either. It's senseless. Most of the things we worry about seldom happen, and they are seldom as bad as we imagine. So quit worrying and start living!

One day at a time!

8.

Live It Up . . . by Living Right
A Clear Conscience

When Hurricane Donna cut a wide path of destruction across Central Florida in 1960, our family lived just south of Apopka on Highway 441. Our subdivision home was near Lake Pleasant. The hurricane rains caused the lake to flood, and people evacuated their houses on the backside of the lake.

Having nothing particular to do, a buddy of mine and I drove down to the lake and went out in our rowboat. We ended up at the flooded houses. He had been over there the day before and had gone in an old house. He had broken out some of the light bulbs. We rationalized that no one would come back to live in this old house, so we broke the mirror in the medicine cabinet door. Next, we broke some windows out. Everything was "cool" until we went out the door. A man came up and asked what we were doing. After warning us about how much trouble we were in, he wrote our names and addresses and said he was going to notify the owner.

I felt really bad about what we had done. I wished we hadn't gotten into the boat and gone over to the flooded-out houses. I worried about the home owner calling my parents. A few days later a patrol car drove slowly through the neighborhood. I just knew the patrolman was going to stop at my house. I felt so guilty. For years, I didn't want to go near the houses that had been flooded. I feared I would be recognized as one of the boys who had done the destruction.

A guilty conscience is hard to live with. It will make one miserable. The voice of excessive guilt will gnaw upon one's conscience night and day.

On the other hand, a clear conscience will help one to sleep well. A French proverb says it like this: "A clear conscience is the softest pillow."

Furthermore, a clear conscience will set one free to enjoy life. It will permit the flow of happiness within one without self-incrimination.

A clear conscience is an essential ingredient in personal happiness. "A cheerful heart does good like medicine, but a broken spirit makes one sick" (Prov. 17:22, TLB).

Most would admit it is far easier to talk about a clear conscience than to have one. To achieve a clear conscience you must properly handle your excessive guilt and live right to keep it.

How to Handle Excessive Guilt

Few human emotions are as distressing and painful as feelings of guilt. Unless one handles them properly, they are very destructive. Excessive guilt will not go away by itself. I suggest you do four things to clear your conscience if you are experiencing feelings of guilt.

Own Up to It

First, own up to wrong deeds. If you did wrong, admit that you did it. It is easier to confess to doing wrong than to keep silent and let it gnaw on your conscience continually.

"A preacher of the early 1900s said that when he was 12 years old he had killed one of the family geese by throwing a stone and hitting it squarely on the head. Figuring his parents wouldn't notice that one of the 24 birds was missing, he buried the dead fowl. But that evening his sister called him aside and said, 'I saw what you did. If you don't offer to do the dishes tonight, I'll tell mother.' The next morning she gave him the same warning. All that day and the next, the frightened boy felt bound to do the dishes. The following morning, however, he surprised his sister by telling her it was her turn. When she quietly reminded him of what she could do, he replied, 'I've already told Mother, and she has forgiven me. Now you do the dishes. I'm free again!' " [1] Face up to your wrong. It's better to face up to wrong actions than to run from them.

Make Restitution Where Possible

Second, make restitution for wrong deeds where possible. Confessing your wrong is important, but it is also necessary to make things right if you can. If you have stolen something, return it. If you have taken money, pay it back.

If you shoplifted a purse from Wal-Mart, took tools from an oil company, turned in more hours than you worked, or if you cheated on your taxes, you must make restitution, or your conscience will gnaw on you. You won't be able to shut it up until you return what you stole and until you pay back what you received wrongfully. If it is where you can do so, making restitution will help you to clear your conscience.

Apologize for Misdeeds and Words

Third, if you have wronged someone, apologize for your misdeeds or words. "I'm sorry," "I was wrong," "Please forgive me" are hard words to say to someone you have wronged. It takes a big person to apologize.

Even if you weren't at fault, or you felt you did no wrong, you should apologize to try to straighten out the problem or misunderstanding. In this case your apology could be like this, "I didn't mean to hurt you by my actions (or what I said). I'm sorry your feelings were hurt. I want our friendship to be strong, even though we may disagree." It's important that you do your best to straighten out any situation where you have hurt someone else.

Go to the person immediately. Try to settle your differences before hard feelings fester into bitterness, resentment, and possibly revenge. It's much easier to put out a spark than a raging fire.

If the hurt party will not accept your apology, you can't do anything more except to pray for them. Knowing you have done all you can do to correct the wrong, you can have peace of mind about its outcome. Having done your best, you can sleep with your actions.

Confess Your Sins to God

Fourth, confess your sins to God. He will forgive. The Bible says, "If we confess our sins, he is faithful and just to forgive us our sins, and to cleanse us from all unrighteousness" (1 John 1:9).

Jesus teaches us to empty our hearts daily of every known sin. In the Lord's Prayer, Jesus teaches us to pray, "Give us this day our daily bread. . . . And lead us not into temptation, but deliver us from evil" (Matt. 6:11,13). He taught us to ask for our bread (needs) and for guidance and protection daily. Sandwiched in between, Jesus taught us to pray, "And forgive us our debts, as we forgive our debtors" (v. 12). Just as we are pray for bread, for guidance, and for protection daily, we are to ask for forgiveness daily.

When you've asked God to forgive you, accept His forgiveness as an accomplished fact. John said, "If we confess our sins, he is faithful and just to forgive" (1 John 1:9). God does not go back on His word or lie. He is "faithful and just" to do what He said He would do.

God not only forgives our sins: He forgets them when we

turn from them and ask His forgiveness. In Jeremiah 31:34*a* our Lord promises, "I will forgive their iniquity, and I will remember their sin no more." Frank Pollard expounds the verse like this: "God has placed our sins in the sea of his forgetfulness and has put up a sign: 'No Fishing Here.'"[2]

Also, you must learn to forgive yourself as God forgives you. Sometimes it's easier to forgive others than to forgive ourselves. But no useful purpose is served by relentless self-condemnation. After asking for and receiving God's forgiveness, forgive yourself. Put it behind you, and go on with your life. Be like Paul, "Forgetting what is behind and straining toward what is ahead" (Phil. 3:13*b*). If you can't come to terms with yourself after a reasonable length of time, you should seek professional help to enable you to call a halt to your excessive guilt.

To resolve your guilt, own up to wrong deeds, make restitution wherever possible, apologize for misdeeds and words, and confess your sins to God. Removing the barriers of guilt that imprison your joy will let happiness flow freely in your life. Now that we have looked at ways to clear your conscience, let's think about how to keep it clear.

Always Try to Do Right

Consider the consequences of your actions before you act. Many things look exciting and appealing, but not everything is good for you. The effects of doing wrong are far reaching, so always try to do right.

Doing wrong always costs more than you think. It starts so innocently. A woman wrote to syndicated columnist Ann Landers about an affair she had with a guy she talked to on the CB. They met for a quick lunch. The "chemistry" was right. The quick lunch turned into a five-hour stay in a nearby motel. Afterwards, she regretted what she had done. She confessed, "When I got home and started to fix supper, I felt so ashamed

I'd like to have died. The guilt is killing me, but I'm afraid to confess it to my husband. It will ruin our marriage." She signed the letter—"Feeling Rotten in MD."[3] When we realize the consequences of our foolish actions, it is often too late. Almost always, doing wrong costs us more than we intended to pay.

Doing wrong not only costs us more than we want to pay, it also keeps us longer than we wanted to stay. A Colorado man wrote, "Dear Ann Landers: My wife and I went to high school together in the '50s. A month or so after a big July Fourth weekend she whispered the magic words, 'I'm pregnant.' So, like all the jerks of that era, I married her. I figured on getting out later, but our son was retarded, and I just couldn't leave.

"So what happens now? My life is more than half over, and I'm an unfulfilled, middle-aged man. I was never able to do the things I wanted to do because I was stuck in a business owned by my in-laws. I suspect my wife feels as trapped as I do.

"I did grow to care for her and the boy, but I can't help but wonder what I missed because of one reckless night. By the way, I was not her 'first,' but she was mine. I've had a few minor affairs over the years and one that was serious, but I couldn't marry the woman because of circumstances.

"Let this be a lesson to your impetuous readers. Think of the long-term consequences before you jump in the sack. I wish I had.—Signed, Daydreaming in Colorado."[4] Stop and think before acting. Doing wrong will keep you longer than you want to stay.

"Everybody's doing it!" has become a common excuse for doing wrong. It's so easy to come to think if everyone is "going all the way," cheating, lying, gambling, getting drunk, cussing, or having an affair, it somehow makes it OK. First, everyone is not doing it. And second, even if they were it wouldn't make it right.

God gave us the standard for right living a long time ago. His rules for moral conduct are the Ten Commandments. They teach us not to worship other gods or make graven images or use God's name in vain. We are to remember the sabbath day and honor our parents. Also, we are not to kill, commit adultery, steal, or covet (Ex. 20:1-17). What once was wrong is still wrong.

You may be thinking, "Everything isn't black and white. There are a lot of things in the grey area that are hard to decide if doing them would be harmful or not." T. B. Maston in his book *Right or Wrong?* gave us some practical help in this area. He suggested three tests to help us decide whether or not something is right or wrong for us. The first test is that of *secrecy*. When deciding, ask yourself, "Are there some individuals whom I would not want to know about this thing if I do it?" Would you want your mother, your Sunday School teacher, or your best friend to know you smoked marijuana, stole the test answers, or told a coarse joke?

The second test is that of *universality*. "Would it be all right with me if everyone else did this same thing?" You may quickly say, "Sure, it's OK with me." But what if your best friend, pastor, or school teacher did it? Would you be horrified? If everyone was doing it, would it make our community or town or nation a better place in which to live?

The third test is that of *prayer*. Ask yourself, "Can I pray about it? Can I ask God to go with me? Can I ask God to bless me in doing it?"[5] If something passes these three tests, you can be confident that it is right for you.

You don't have to "go along" to "get along." Don't be afraid to be different. Doing right can be achieved only through exercising an ever-vigilant self-control. It will require maturity and wise discretion. The effort put forth always to do right will pay a priceless dividend of a clear conscience.

"Live It Up" Doing Right

Some feel we don't have any fun unless we get into trouble. But that's not true. This misconception partly comes from so many Christians, especially preachers, acting too stiff and formal in social situations. They have paraded flamboyantly their negative virtues so long until others see them as not having any fun. We can "live it up" doing right.

A case in point: John Drakeford served as a chaplain during World War II. His first test came when the colonel met him at the club, introduced him to his fellow officers, then jovially asked, "How about a whiskey?"

"Thank you, sir, but I don't drink."

As they stood chatting, a major offered him a cigarette. "I appreciate it, but I don't smoke."

About that time a bright-eyed lieutenant came rushing up. "Hi! Say, you're new here, aren't you? We are having a dance on Saturday night and need another man to escort one of the nurses. How about it?"

"Sorry, I don't dance," Drakeford gulped.

"Chaplain," spoke a captain who had been observing all this, "do you spit?"[6]

A negative, austere attitude that rains on everybody's party is contrary to the joy-filled life Jesus intended for us. He said, "I am come that they might have life and that they might have it more abundantly" (John 10:10). He promised His followers a superabundant life. The new life He gives is not highlighted with negative virtues but instead is characterized by positive living.

Doing right can be plenty of fun. Ever since I started going to church regularly as a teenager, I have tried to do what was right, and I have had plenty of good times along the way. At youth fellowships, we played rhythm, fruit-basket turnover, and charades. We did a lot of singing, eating, and laughing. Those fellowships were tremendous fun.

College days were fun, too. I studied especially hard during my two years at Mississippi College. Many nights I would study at the library until it closed, then study in the old science building until eleven or so. Then when I returned to the dormitory, I was ready to tease, joke around, and socialize. It was fun. I usually stayed up late with some of the fellows. Sometimes, I was up late cramming for a test. I often dozed in class. My friends kidded me as being the only one in New Testament Survey who could go to sleep before the roll sheet was passed around. I remember waking up from a Mississippi history class and being the only one left in the room. I'll bet I was a comical sight in my seat at the front of the class "sawing logs." I studied hard and played hard. Every minute at Mississippi College was fun for me, even the time I accidentally threw a snowball through the dean of women's office window!

I looked forward to the BSU ministry trips. A group of students, usually six or eight of us, would go to the county men's home, rescue mission, jail, or the children's hospital to visit the people and conduct a worship service. We would sing choruses at the top of our lungs in that van coming and going. We felt like we were helping others who needed a smile and a visit, and we had a good time doing it, too.

As newlyweds, Violet and I went to the Golden Gate Baptist Theological Seminary located just north of the Golden Gate Bridge on the San Francisco Bay. In many ways, it was tough and challenging. We wouldn't take anything for the experiences we had riding the cable cars, freezing at a Giants' baseball game in Candlestick Park, salmon fishing in the Pacific, driving through the Redwood forests, spending the night in an old logging town hotel in McCloud, snow sledding in the Sierras, sightseeing in Yosemite National Park, seeing the Pebble Beach golf course in Monterey, touring Hearst Castle at San Simeon, going to Hollywood and Disneyland, and seeing Nixon's home at San Clemente.

Seminary was filled with good experiences—one I remember quite vividly. I was in Dr. Francis DuBose's missions class right after lunch. It's hard to stay awake after one has just eaten, especially with the sun shining through the window. Most classes passed around a roll chart on which students marked themselves present for the day. Occasionally, someone would mark you present before the roll got to you. Nobody seemed to mind. In the class was Alice Hyatt. She was of retirement age. Her late husband had been the librarian at the seminary for years. She was taking the missions class along with the rest of us. Sherman Glenn and I decided to mark her present before the chart reached her. When the sheet came to her, she would line up her name and the column for that day's attendance. Seeing a check mark in her spot, she would double check to make sure she had found the proper spot to check. Realizing somebody had marked her present, she would slowly turn around to figure out who had done it. This went on for days. Sherman and I were enjoying it.

Finally, one day, she raised her hand and asked Dr. DuBose to please send the roll chart around to her side of the room first since someone was marking her present before the chart came to her. Sherman and I were having too good of a time to let it drop, so we began marking her name a day ahead! Everyday she went through the same ritual. She'd get her pencil out of her purse, line her name up with the column, and prepare to mark herself present. After double checking and making sure that her spot had already been marked, she would slowly look around the room trying to figure who would have marked her name again.

Sherman and I were laughing so hard that finally Dr. DuBose spoke out, "I don't know what's wrong with you two fellows, but you are disrupting the class everyday. I want to see you in my office after class." So Sherman and I went to the professor's office to explain the situation. He straightened it out, but we had a good time with Mrs. Hyatt and the roll chart. We also grew up.

We don't have to get into trouble to "live it up." We can "live it up" doing right. When we have clean fun, we don't have to worry about our consciences hurting us afterwards. Clean fun is the best fun of all.

Getting It All Together

A guilty conscience is hard to live with. Carrying a burden of guilt will take the joy and zest out of life. But a clear conscience will free you to enjoy life.

Few human emotions are as distressing and painful as feelings of guilt. To resolve guilt one should:

1. *Own up to wrong deeds.* If you did wrong, own up to it. It's better to confess to being the culprit than to keep silent and let it gnaw on your conscience continually.

2. *Make restitution for wrong deeds wherever possible.* Confessing your wrong is important, but it is also necessary to make things right if you can. If you stole something, return it. If you broke something, fix it or pay for it. If you received overpayment, return it. If you cheated Uncle Sam, pay what you owe. Everything you can make right, you should.

3. *Apologize for your misdeeds and words.* When you hurt someone, go to that person immediately and apologize. Even if you felt you weren't at fault, you can apologize for the hardship or hurt you caused them, if you didn't mean to hurt them. It isn't easy to apologize, but doing so will straighten out a lot of fractured relationships.

4. *Confess your sins to God.* He will forgive you. Each day you should empty your heart of the sins you committed. When you sincerely ask for God's forgiveness, accept His forgiveness as an accomplished fact. He promises to forgive us when we ask, and God does not lie. Also, forgive yourself. No useful purpose is served by relentless self-condemnation.

To keep your conscience clear, you should *always try to do right*. Consider the consequences of your actions before you act. Doing wrong has far-reaching effects. It always costs you more than you think and keeps you longer than you want to stay.

Doing right can be achieved only through exercizing an ever-vigilant self-control. It requires maturity and wise discretion. It requires constant effort, but the priceless dividends of a clear conscience are worth it.

Some feel you can't have any fun unless you get into trouble. But it isn't true. *You can "live it up" doing right*. Doing right can be lots of fun. An added bonus of clean fun is: we don't have to try to live down a guilty conscience afterwards.

Conclusion

Happiness is no secret. It's found in the simplest shacks to the most elegant mansions. The elements that bring happiness are:

1. *A good self-image*. A low self-esteem will hold one down throughout life unless one works to change it.

2. *A fulfilling work*. Don't hesitate to work hard, for some of the greatest happiness you will ever experience will come from your work.

3. *A generous spirit*. If we give generously without thought of getting anything in return, there is no limit to the happiness that will come to us.

4. *A grateful heart*. A person who is thankful for what he or she has lives a happier life than an ungrateful person.

5. *A spiritual life*. A restless inner void exists in our hearts until we fill it with God.

6. *A helping hand*. Looking out just for "number one" leads to misery while helping others adds to happiness.

7. *A positive outlook*. It is not what happens to us that determines our degree of happiness but how we handle it.

8. *A clear conscience*. It will permit the flow of happiness within without self-incrimination.

You may be thinking, *If these eight elements are the secret to happiness, then, I'll just change my ways a little bit to include them, and I'll be happy.* The thing wrong with that kind of thinking is it doesn't take into consideration our selfish nature. We all tend to be self-centered.

Selfishness is a spiritual problem. Only Christ can take away a selfish attitude and replace it with love for others. By imitating Christ, we can learn to love others unconditionally.

Achieving happiness is paradoxical. We get it by giving. We may selfishly seek comfort and wealth and attain them, but we won't be happy. Why? Because we were not created to grasp ease and security but to serve God and to help our fellow human beings.

A cautious, self-centered approach to life is not life at all. The person who faces life, risks all for God and others. Let love control your actions, and you will experience untold happiness.

The elements of happiness I have described in this book are not definitive. One could cite other contributing factors, but these are the primary ones. It is my prayer that you will have more happiness than you ever dreamed of as you include these elements in your life.

Notes

Chapter 1—*The Real You Is Trying to Come Out*

1. Kenneth L. Chafin, sermon, *The Pulpit of Walnut Street Baptist Church,* No. 30, Vol. XV (Louisville, KY: Walnut Street Baptist Church, August 9, 1984).

2. Lee Stoller, *One Day at a Time* (Madison, TN: LS Records, 1983), pp. 15-17,51-52.

3. Bill Stephens, "Self-worth: Everyone Needs It," No. 6, Vol. XI (Atlanta, GA: *The North Peachtree Baptist Messenger,* North Peachtree Baptist Church, August, 1985), p. 4.

4. Martin R. DeHaan II, "Of Turkeys and Dodos," *Our Daily Bread,* ed. Dennis J. DeHaan, Sept.-Oct. 1985 (Grand Rapids, MI: Radio Bible Class, Oct. 13, 1985).

5. Frank Pollard, sermon, "Your Future Is Ahead of You," broadcast on "The Baptist Hour," May 20, 1983.

6. Wayne Dehoney, *The Pulpit of Walnut Street Baptist Church,* No. 39, Vol. XII (Louisville, KY: Walnut Street Baptist Church, Sept. 24, 1981), p. 3.

7. Jules Lot, "Contest Lady Doesn't Miss Challenges," *The Gleaner* (Henderson, KY), May 1, 1981, p. 17.

8. Lionel Crocker, "Life in These United States," *Reader's Digest* (Pleasantville, NY: The Reader's Digest Association, Nov. 1974), pp. 121-122.

9. Douglas Naugler, "Nothing to Do," *The Upper Room Daily Devotional Guide,* July-Aug. 1985 (Nashville: The Upper Room, August 12), p. 51.

10. "Youth Earns Law Degree at Age 16," *The Gleaner,* Ibid., Dec. 31, 1985, p. A-10.

Chapter 2—*Between Lunch and Breaks*

1. Earl Nightingale, film, *The Strangest Secret,* Nightingale & Conant, 1970.

2. Harry Tassel, "Personal Glimpses," *Reader's Digest,* Feb. 1985, p. 119.

3. Joyce Brothers, *How to Get Whatever You Want Out of Life* (New York: Simon & Schuster, 1978), pp. 4-7.

4. Frank Pollard, "Keep Growing," broadcast on "The Baptist Hour," January 4, 1985.

5. Brian L. Harbour, *From Cover to Cover* (Nashville: Broadman Press, 1982), p. 204.

6. Jimmy Carter, *Why Not the Best?* (Nashville: Broadman Press, 1975), p. 59.

7. Carl Holmes, "And Then Some," *Pulpit Helps,* ed. Spiros Zodhiates, Vol. 18, Sept. 1985.

8. Jacob M. Braude, *Lifetime Speaker's Encyclopedia,* Vol. II (Englewood Cliffs, NJ: Prentice-Hall, Inc., 1962), p. 1107.

9. Frank Bettger, *How I Multiplied My Income and Happiness in Selling* (Englewood Cliffs, NJ: Prentice-Hall, Inc., 1961), pp. 9-10.

10. William Novak, "Iacocca" in "Personal Glimpses," *Reader's Digest,* March 1985, p. 31.

11. Charles L. Allen, *God's Psychiatry* (Fleming H. Revell Co., 1953), p. 57.

12. *Our Daily Bread,* Ibid., Sept.-Oct. 1985.

13. Charles Allen, Ibid., p. 58.

14. *Pulpit Helps,* "Bulletin Inserts," Sept. 1985, p. 36.

Chapter 3—*All I Have to Offer You Is Me*

1. Joyce Brothers, Ibid., pp. 17-18.

2. *Growing in the Grace of Giving,* tract printed in the USA by the Stewardship Commission of the Southern Baptist Convention, Nashville, TN.

3. William Barclay, *The Gospel of Luke, The Daily Study Bible* (Philadelphia: The Westminster Press, 1956), p. 168.

4. Frank Pollard, "Are You Independently Wealthy?, broadcast on "The Baptist Hour," Sept. 2, 1983, No. BH36-83.

5. Wayne Dehoney, "Getting What You Want in Life," from *The Pulpit of Walnut Street Baptist Church,* No. 41, Vol. XII, Oct. 8, 1981.

6. *Tithe . . . I Challenge You,* tract printed in the USA by the Stewardship Commission of the Southern Baptist Convention, No. NST 676.

7. Charles Wallis, "Love Ever Gives," *Selected Poems of John Oxenham* (New York: Harper & Bros., 1948), p. 84.

8. Erich Bridges, "Physician Paid in Different Currency," *The Baptist Record,* Don McGregor, ed., Jackson, MS, March 10, 1983, p. 3.

Chapter 4—*Thanksgiving and Thanksliving*

1. Edward Ziegler, "Happiness: Who Has It, and Why," *Reader's Digest,* July 1979, p. 78.

2. Wayne Dehoney, "The Gratitude Attitude," from *The Pulpit of Walnut Street Baptist Church,* No. 47, Vol. XV, Nov. 22, 1984.

3. Robert K. Merton, "Points to Ponder," *Reader's Digest,* Mar. 1985, p. 180.

4. *Pulpit Helps,* "Illustrations," Nov. 1985, p. 25.

5. Nancy Brandenberger, "Blessings Should Be Counted," *Pulpit Helps,* No. 2, Vol. 11, Nov. 1985, p. 4.

6. Richard W. DeHaan, "How to Be a Healthy Christian," booklet, Radio Bible Class, 1985, p. 22.

7. Ibid.

Chapter 5—*Filling the Void Inside*

1. Emil Brunner, *The Christian Doctrine of Creation and Redemption—Dogmatics,* Vol. II, translated by Olive Wyon (Philadelphia: The Westminster Press, 1952), p. 127.

2. "Passenger's Joke Results in Lawsuit," *The Gleaner,* Ibid., Jan. 12, 1985, p. A-10, and "Woman Wins $10,000 in Joke Suit," *The Gleaner,* Jan. 17, 1985, p. A-10.

3. Irving D. Larson, "Proud About What?"—from Friendship Baptist Church bulletin, Modesto, CA, 1974, p. 4.

4. Alton Fammin, sermon, "A Missions-Minded Look at Salvation," *Proclaim,* The Sunday School Board of the Southern Baptist Convention, Oct.-Dec. 1985, p. 24.

5. "Decide Today," tract, The Sunday School Board of the Southern Baptist Convention.

6. John Wesley White, "Not Ashamed of the Gospel: For It Is . . ." (Minneapolis, MN: The Billy Graham Evangelistic Association, 1972), p. 14.

Chapter 6—*Help Yourself . . . by Helping Others*
1. Rosalynn Carter, *First Lady from Plains* (Boston: Houghton Mifflin Co., 1984), p. 286.

2. Michelle Randolph, "Happiness: How to Find It," No. 2, Vol. 11, Atlanta, GA, Mar. 1985, p. 7.

3. Annie Johnson Flint, poem printed in *Poems for Daily Needs,* ed. Thomas C. Clark (New York: Round Table Press, 1936), p. 138.

4. E. J. Daniels, sermon, "Going the Second Mile" (Orlando, FL: Christ for the World Publishers), pp. 21-22.

5. "Engage in What You Remember," reprinted in *Pulpit Helps,* July 1985, p. 15.

6. William Marshall, "One Mission Together," *Western Recorder* (KY), ed. Jack D. Sanford, No. 3, Vol. 159, Jan. 22, 1985.

7. Wayne Dehoney, sermon, "Usefulness—The Secret of Happiness II," from *The Pulpit of Walnut Street Baptist Church,* No. 46, Vol. XIII, Nov. 18, 1982.

8. "Bulletin Inserts," *Pulpit Helps,* No. 1, Vol. 10, Jan. 1985, p. 23.

9. Nancy Collins, "Personal Glimpses," *Reader's Digest,* June 1984, p. 186.

Chapter 7—*A Positive Outlook*
1. E. J. Daniels, *"What's Right About the Church?, Christ for the World Family Magazine,* Oct.-Dec. 1981, p. 4.

2. Mark Snowden, "Scan Lives," Cooperative Communications,

Kentucky Baptist Convention Media Department Update, No. 1, Vol. 3, Jan.-Feb. 1986, p. 2.

3. Charles L. Allen, quoted in *The Treasure Chest,* ed. Charles L. Wallis (New York: Harper & Row, Publishers, 1965), p. 80.

4. Pamphlet, *Louis Braille* (New York; American Foundation for the Blind, Inc., Sept. 1979), pp. 4-8.

5. Clint Bonner, *A Hymn Is Born* (Chicago: Wilcox & Follett, Co., 1952), p. 64.

6. Landrum P. Leavell II, sermon, "The Gospel and Those Who Are Helpless," preached at the 1985 Kentucky Baptist Evangelism Conference.

7. Kenneth L. Chafin, sermon, "What to Do with the Down Periods of Your Life," from *The Pulpit of Walnut Street Baptist Church,* No. 11, Vol. XVI, Mar. 22, 1985.

8. Wayne Dehoney, sermon, "When Life Goes to Pieces," from *The Pulpit of Walnut Street Baptist Church,* No. 49, Vol. XV, Dec. 6, 1984, p. 4.

9. Lee Stoller, Ibid., p. 219.

Chapter 8—*Living It Up . . . by Living Right*

1. *Our Daily Bread,* ed. Dennis J. DeHaan, Radio Bible Class, Sept.-Oct. 1985, Vol. 30, No. 6,7.

2. Frank Pollard, *After You've Said I'm Sorry* (Nashville: Broadman Press, 1982), p. 159.

3. Ann Landers, "Confess CB Affair to Clergyman," *The Gleaner,* Feb. 4, 1986, p. B-2.

4. Ann Landers, "Consider Consequences Before Having Children," *The Gleaner,* Sept. 7, 1985, p. B-5.

5. T. B. Maston, *Right or Wrong?* (Nashville: Broadman Press, 1955), pp. 35-39.

6. John W. Drakeford, *Marriage, How to Keep a Good Thing Growing* (Nashville: Impact Books, 1979), pp. 19-20.